At a time when there is a startling and well-documented gap between environmental talk and lifestyle walk, Ruth Valerio is a true pioneer. She has made a humble and practical journey in caring for creation through years of trial and error, and her book allows us to understand the grateful relationship with God which has been the lifespring of her different and creative way of living. L is for Lifestyle brings us all the benefit of Ruth's hard-won experience and applied faith, and will be an essential resource for all who are concerned to live the whole of their lives to God's glory, and for the healing of his creation.

Peter Harris
International Director of A Rocha

Here it is:- hooked-on-phonics for Christian activists. This is an incredible textbook for changing the world, sort of Revolution 101. As with most prophets, Ruth was ahead of the times (hence the 'revised' edition here). But this book is bound to be a guide for the contemporary Church that is increasingly aware that our faith in the God of heaven has to affect the way we live on earth.

Shane Claiborne
Author, activist, and recovering sinner

We rely on Ruth for her readiness to tell it as it is, and urge us to action. We owe her much for the way she brings us back to our calling and responsibilities. This book takes us even further, offering a challenge that none of us can ignore. Buy it, read it, and make a difference.

Elaine Storkey
Theologian and social scientist

A wealth of ideas for those who want to live with integrity in the light of scripture.

Roy McCloughry
Director of The Kingdom Trust

'L' is for
Lifestyle

INTER-VARSITY PRESS
Email: ivp@ivpbooks.com
Website: www.ivpbooks.com

New edition

First published 2004

British Library Cataloguing-in-Publication Data
A catalogue record for this book is available from the British Library.
ISBN 978-1-84474-343-8

Set in Monotype Dante 12/15pt
Typeset in Great Britain by Servis Filmsetting Ltd, Stockport, Cheshire
Printed and bound in Great Britain by Ashford Colour Press Ltd, Gosport, Hampshire

Inter-Varsity Press publishes Christian books that are true to the Bible and that communicate the gospel, develop discipleship and strengthen the church for its mission in the world.

Inter-Varsity Press is closely linked with the Universities and Colleges Christian Fellowship, a student movement connecting Christian Unions in universities and colleges throughout Great Britain, and a member movement of the International Fellowship of Evangelical Students.
Website: *www.uccf.org.uk*

Ruth Valerio

ivp

This book is printed on Forest Stewardship Council certified paper, which contains pulp from responsibly managed forests to ensure the future of communities and the environment.

In addition the paper of this book has been offset with Climate Stewards by planting new forest in Ghana to absorb carbon dioxide, support local communities and provide habitats for wildlife. Climate Stewards is a project of A Rocha. www.climatestewards.net

CONTENTS

INTRODUCTION TO REVISED EDITION

'But you've only just written it!' said a friend of mine when I told her I was revising my book. I have to confess to a certain degree of surprise myself when IVP approached me about revising it: to me, 'revised editions' happen to the likes of John Stott and Ron Sider when their bestsellers have been going for 20-odd years, not to a book that was only published four years ago!

But, we live in a fast-changing world and a lot can happen in four years. Perhaps the starkest change is that, when this book was published in February 2004, there were no fairtrade products in British supermarkets. That made me realise that it was, indeed, time to revise the book!

As I look back over these four years, I see that changes have taken place in three particular areas. The first of these is global. One of the most notable features of our world is the phenomenal economic growth experienced by China, as also by India and Brazil.(1) Together, their growing energy demands will account for around 42% of the total projected increase in world energy demand. The environmental consequences of this economic growth, along with an abysmal human rights record, have not gone unnoticed. Of the world's 30 most polluted cities 20 are in China, now the largest energy consumer in the world. In a book on personal lifestyle changes, these facts must not be overlooked and we must take every available opportunity to push for global responses.

Another notable global feature is the way that perceptions of climate change have altered. When first writing 'E is for Energy', I felt the need to write a brief description of what climate change is; now that's not necessary! Alongside the 'war on terror', economic issues and the Beckhams, human-induced ('anthropogenic') climate change is a highly profiled issue in the media. The debates around its veracity are largely decided and finished: the current debate is how to deal with the changes that will inevitably happen, and how we can reduce our carbon dioxide (CO_2) emissions to stop it accelerating out of control. Climate change has become *the* issue facing us today, to the extent that I could almost re-name this book, *C is for Climate Change*, because the majority of what I examine in this book impacts on, and is impacted by, climate change.

It astounds me how incredibly slowly we are, as individuals and as nations, responding to this issue, compared to the swift response that was taken after 9/11, both financially and politically. Our grandchildren will certainly ask us some hard-hitting and incredulous questions as to why on earth we continued living as we did when we knew what we knew. I hope I don't give the impression in this book that all we need to do is shop a bit more ethically and then we have 'done our bit'. The reality is that those of us living in the more economically developed countries must be prepared to limit our lifestyles, and radically. With Europe and America between them being responsible for more than 90% of the emissions that are already in the atmosphere, we are surely the ones who have to make the sacrifices.

The second area where change has occurred is in the church's response to the need to care for God's world, particularly in the UK, although things are changing in America too. It is no surprise that, as society as a whole has been waking up to the state of our world, so the Church has been too, and we have been wrestling with how to respond *as Christians.* All the major denominations in the UK have brought out statements on creation care, and looking after God's world is no longer seen as a slightly weird thing, but as an important part of Christian living today. Our understanding and verbal assent are however still largely divorced from our action. My prayer is that this book will continue to play its part in bringing the two together.

The third area where I see change is in myself. In the Introduction to the first edition I wrote, 'this book comes from my own journey through these issues'. Well, that journey hasn't stopped! I have kept trying, step by step, to find new ways of living that do as little damage as possible to God's world and its inhabitants, humans of course included.

To discuss all those different steps would be somewhat boring and self-obsessive, but what excite me most (and seem to interest others most too) are my attempts at growing and rearing some of my own food. Like many people, I now have an allotment, which I share with friends and from which we derive an inordinate amount of pleasure (and certainly out of all proportion to what we manage to produce!). Like a growing number of people, I keep chickens in the back garden to provide eggs. With some friends again, I now rear pigs, hence producing my own fresh pork, sausages, bacon and ham. The pigs are kept in a field belonging to a residential centre for adults with learning difficulties and the people at the centre help us look after the pigs (and, of course, eat the finished product!). The whole experience has been great for adults and children alike, and it has become such a wonderful part of our lives that my husband, Greg, jokes about me writing a book entitled, *P is for Pigs*! It has been exciting doing all this, thanks partly to fantastic friends who have become as equally committed as me to these things, while still living in a terraced house on our council estate.

So the journey towards sustainable living never ends. Even now, while writing this, Greg and I are in discussion about selling our car and buying an electric G-wizz car, and I am currently experimenting with washing our clothes with Indian nuts (no joke! Check out www.soapods.com. So far they seem to be working). I am also getting involved in the Transition Towns initiative and the concept of peak oil. I hope that this book encourages you to keep going on the journey, and to discover that it is demanding, fun and best done with other people.

Many of us are deeply concerned with the problems of injustice and poverty that are so prevalent in our world. We recognize that our lives are interlinked with those of other people around the world. We already give to various charities, but want to do more with our lifestyles to make those links beneficial rather than detrimental. The scale of the issues often seems overwhelming, however, leading to a sense of hopelessness. We do not know where to start. This book aims to break down the issues into manageable, bite-sized chunks, and to give very practical pointers to possible responses.

You may be new to these issues, but keen to learn more about what is happening and take some first steps. You may be doing lots already and need some fresh ideas. You may be a student wanting to know what lifestyle options you can adopt when you graduate. You may want to know how to juggle the demands of a young family and mortgage repayments and still be a Christian actively concerned with wider global issues. Perhaps you are well established in life, with children at university and a good income (and a matching credit-card bill!) coming in every month, and yet you still want to know how to use the things God has blessed you with to bless others. You might now be retired, or maybe you have been made redundant, and you want to discover how to use your time to make a difference. Perhaps you are just exhausted with the pressures of consumerism and you want to explore the possibilities of a simpler lifestyle.

There are many things we can do to make a difference, and this book gives suggestions for minor changes as well as major challenges. Whatever your situation, you will find things to encourage and inspire you. Conversely, your particular situation may also mean that there are aspects of this book that you cannot take on. The aim is definitely not to make you feel guilty! Try taking a step-by-step approach, doing one or two things first, rather than taking on all the action points at once. When they become a part of your normal life, then do some more. This is a book to come back to again and again, dipping into different chapters as you wish.

As mentioned above, it will be obvious as you read on that this book comes from my own journey. I have become increasingly aware of the problems that our world is facing, and concerned that, as a follower of Jesus, I have to play my part in doing something about them. The book therefore arises from my own circumstances – that is, normal life! I don't live up a mountain in total self-sufficiency; I live on a council estate with two young children, a mortgage, and the stress of supermarket shopping. Lots of this book I am living already, and I hope I am an encouraging example of the fact that it can be done. There are parts of this book, though, where the suggested action is still an aspiration for me. For those of you who know me well, I ask you to be kind to me! Because it comes from my own journey, this book contains a lot of my personal opinions and stories. There will no doubt be things that you disagree with or other ways of achieving the same ends. I hope that you will find your own way through the pointers that this book provides.

Each chapter ends, where appropriate, with action points and additional references. Please check out the website, www.lisforlifestyle.com, which accompanies this book where you will find suggestions for further reading, organisations to contact for further information, and the full bibliography.

I want to thank those people who have helped with *L is for Lifestyle*. Roy McCloughry gave a great deal of time to working through the manuscript, and to helping me, as a first-time author, to get the book into a publishable state. A massive 'thank you' to him. The Friends of the Earth Information Service has consistently replied to my questions with detailed and helpful answers. Thank you, also, to Tim Bushell, Michael Lomotey, Bev Thomas, and my parents Martin and Elizabeth Goldsmith, who all commented on particular chapters.

Various people and organisations have helped update this second edition and I want to thank them: Chris Davis from the Fairtrade Foundation; Dave Bookless from A Rocha; Bill Guyton from the World Cocoa Foundation; Canon Edmund Newell from St Paul's Cathedral; Friends of the Earth and the Soil Association Information Services; Richard Hunter from Equity Invest; Duncan Green from Oxfam; Abby Dalglish from Banana Link; Nick Spencer from Theos; Professor John Chudleigh from Analysing Agriculture (Australia), and my editor at IVP, Eleanor Trotter.

Finally, this book is dedicated to my wonderful husband, Greg, who first opened my eyes to justice issues and pushed me to write this book; and to my two beautiful children Mali and Jemba. May I inspire in them the love for God's world and his people that my parents inspired in me.

Endnote

1 I am not saying that this has only happened since 2004, but that the significance of this growth is being increasingly recognized and discussed.

A IS FOR ACTIVISTS

One of my most memorable experiences is visiting the Sisters of Charity, Mother Teresa's order, in Addis Ababa, Ethiopia. In that city of incredible poverty, their call is to the very bottom of the heap: to those who are dying and have been abandoned by friends and family. Each morning, the sisters open their compound gates and bring in those who have been abandoned there overnight. The compound is divided into separate rooms for different illnesses, each room containing neat rows of dying people on iron beds – a very unnerving sight.

The sisters themselves follow a rigorous routine. Their day starts at 5am with a set rhythm: practical care for those they are looking after, personal prayer, times of rest and eating and corporate prayer with the other sisters. Through this rhythm, they are given the necessary strength to face the day's demands.

Few of us are called to lead the life of these sisters. Yet all of us in different ways are called to be activists for God's kingdom. Just consider these well-known words:

'Is not this the kind of fasting I have chosen:
to loose the chains of injustice
and untie the cords of the yoke,
to set the oppressed free
and break every yoke?
Is it not to share your food with the hungry
to provide the poor wanderer with shelter –
when you see the naked, to clothe them,
and not to turn away from your own flesh and blood? . . .
If you do away with the yoke of oppression,
with the pointing finger and malicious talk,
and if you spend yourselves on behalf of the hungry
and satisfy the needs of the oppressed,
then your light will rise in the darkness,
and your night will become like the noonday.'
(Isaiah 58:6–7, 9b–10)

This passage is found in the final part of Isaiah, which describes what Alec Motyer calls 'the characteristics of a waiting people'; a people seeking to live an obedient life while waiting for the Lord. The previous verses (2–5) describe the kind of fasting that God rejects. It is fasting that tries to manipulate a response from God (compare 1 Kings 18:16–29) but actually leads only to exploitation and fights. Instead of using the time freed up by fasting for meaningless rituals (verse 5), the time should be spent working towards a just society (verse 6), taking care of the needs of strangers and family members (verse 7) and ensuring that personal behaviour matches this social response (verses 9–10).

These are hardly passive words; it is impossible to do these things without active involvement in what is happening in the world around us. This book is aimed at helping all who want to spend ourselves on behalf of the hungry and satisfy the needs of the oppressed. We can be activists in many different ways, but whatever we do, we do it in order to see God's righteousness and justice extended into our world.

So let us look further at why we should be activists.

First, we are to be activists because *activism is rooted in the heart and character of God himself*, as Father, Son and Holy Spirit. The Bible tells of a trinitarian God actively involved with his people, working out his plans for the salvation of the whole world. One of the best expressions of God's character is in Psalm 146:

> *He upholds the cause of the oppressed*
> *and gives food to the hungry.*
> *The LORD sets prisoners free,*
> *the LORD gives sight to the blind,*
> *the LORD lifts up those who are bowed down,*
> *the LORD loves the righteous.*
> *The LORD watches over the alien*
> *and sustains the fatherless and the widow,*
> *but he frustrates the ways of the wicked.*
> (Psalm 146:7–9)

God's salvation plans find their fulfilment in the active nature of Jesus, the Son, who came down to this earth as a human being to restore and reconcile the world to God (Romans 8:19–21; 2 Corinthians 5:18–21; Ephesians 2:11–18; Colossians 1:19–20). The incarnation is the ultimate expression of God's compassion as he enters into his creation, taking on our suffering. Jesus' life continues this demonstration of his compassion, and his twin emphasis on the poor and on proclaiming the good news is best captured in what many would see as his manifesto:

The Spirit of the Lord is on me,
because he has anointed me
to preach good news to the poor.
He has sent me to proclaim freedom for the prisoners
and recovery of sight for the blind,
to release the oppressed,
to proclaim the year of the Lord's favour.
(Luke 4:18–19)

Jesus came in order that people 'may have life, and have it to the full' (John 10:10), and he accomplished this by his life, death and resurrection.

Secondly, we are to be activists because *activism is the call that God has placed on us*. Those earlier words from Isaiah 58 make that clear, and so does Micah 6:8:

He has showed you, O people, what is good.
And what does the Lord require of you?
To act justly and to love mercy
and to walk humbly with your God.

So does Proverbs 29:7:

The righteous care about justice for the poor,
but the wicked have no such concern.

Indeed, the way in which the nation of Israel was established demonstrated that God's people were to be different from those around them. One of the main ways was through their treatment of other people and the land that God had created.

They were to look after those who were vulnerable and unable to look after themselves (e.g. Deuteronomy 10:18–19; Exodus 22:22), and laws were established to prevent huge inequalities appearing (e.g. the laws against moving boundary stones, Deuteronomy 19:14; 27:17). The best-known of these laws are the Jubilee laws of Leviticus 25. These recognized that differences in material status would appear, but sought to ensure that limits were imposed. While a person could gain extra land and reap the benefits of the income it brought, that land was eventually to be returned to the original owner at the time of the Jubilee. The foundation for these laws was the experience of Israel's suffering in Egypt and her covenant relationship with a God who has an active love for justice (e.g. Leviticus 25:39–43).

Jesus' parable of the Good Samaritan in Luke 10 similarly urges us to be actively involved with our neighbour. The question asked by the expert in the law is effectively 'Who is my neighbour, whom I should love as myself?' Jesus turns the answer round so that the neighbour is the one doing the active caring (rather than the one who needs to be cared for, as is often presumed), and tells the 'expert': 'Go, then, and *be* that neighbour yourself.' There is no excuse allowed for knowing of someone's distress and doing nothing about it. James emphasizes this too when he stresses that the mark of a religion that is acceptable to God is that we 'look after orphans and widows in their distress and . . . keep [ourselves] from being polluted by the world' (James 1:27).

Just as the Israelites' experience of redemption was the foundation for their care of the poor, so it is Jesus' death for us that gives us the ultimate reason for our calling to be activists on behalf of those in need:

This is how we know what love is: Jesus Christ laid down his life for us. And we ought to lay down our lives for one another. If anyone of you

> *has material possessions and sees a brother or sister in need but has no pity on them, how can the love of God be in you? Dear children, let us not love with words or tongue but with actions and in truth.*
> (1 John 3:16–18)

Thirdly, we are to be activists because *people have been made in the image of God* (Genesis 1:26–27). The fact that this phrase has been debated throughout church history warns us against locating its meaning too narrowly and seeing it as referring exclusively to our rationality or our sense of morality. The phrase has many dimensions (more of which we shall see in 'C is for Creation'). One important dimension is our creation as relational beings, and particularly our ability to have an intimate relationship with God – one of the key things that distinguishes us from the rest of creation. This is wonderfully captured by Augustine, who famously prayed, 'You have made us for yourself, and our hearts are restless until they find their rest in you.' There is a spiritual dimension within us all that is integral to what it means to be human.

This is important in understanding why we should be activists in our world today. It is highlighted by the covenant that God made with Noah and the land, which sees our creation in the image of God as the reason we are accountable for one another (Genesis 9:5–6). So our relationship with God is extended to our relationship with one another. A person who is viewed as just a physical being, devoid of all spiritual orientation, is, in essence, dehumanized. When we lose our true humanity, we must search for it elsewhere; hence the rampant rise of materialism. When we lose our true humanity, we lose our basis for compassion and concern, and that is what leads to the terrible injustices in our world today.

Fourthly, we should be activists because of *the state of our world*. Today, as you read this, 27 000 children under the age of five will die from poverty-related causes and 3000 children will die of malaria. 41% of the population of sub-Saharan Africa live below $1 a day. In Britain 13 million people live on a low income and a quarter of all nineteen year olds lack minimum levels of qualification. In the US, there are 47 million people (15.8% of the population) with no health insurance. Each of these people has been made in the image of God, so how can we remain inactive?

Finally, we are to be activists because of *our hope for the future*. The above statistics make for depressing reading and lead to a sombre recognition that, through the Fall, the world is not as it should be and we shall never sort everything out in the present. The good news of Jesus is that we can look forward to a very different future, one that we begin to experience now through his life, death and resurrection, but that will be brought in fully when he comes again (Ephesians 1:13–14).

The final chapters of Revelation give us a picture of that future, when there will be 'no more death or mourning or crying or pain' (21:4) and when the river of the water of life will flow and the tree of life will bear fruit (22:1–2). It is this future hope that motivates us in our lives today, in the same way that Paul's teaching on the future leads him to encourage us to live a godly life in the present (e.g. 1 Corinthians 15:58; 1 Thessalonians 4:13 – 5:11). In the words of Jürgen Moltmann, 'from first to last, and not merely in the epilogue, Christianity is eschatology, is hope, forward looking and forward moving, and therefore also revolutionizing and transforming the present'.

As we live in the tension between the 'now' that Jesus' first coming has brought and the 'not yet' that will be realized with his second coming, we are to demonstrate an active attitude of 'expectancy and anticipation'. Our role is to be living examples of the future, anticipating now what we know the future holds. In that way, as Bible scholar Bruce Milne says,

Because of the victory Jesus has already achieved by his resurrection, his followers are never driven to despair even when faced with the most appalling social conditions. They are called rather to an active participation in that new movement in history which takes God's intentions and purposes for mankind as their own. However limited or imperfect his impact may be, a Christian 'knows that every stand he takes for social righteousness and every effort he makes towards social renewal and justice and tolerance is not lost'.

What sort of activists, then, should we be?

First, as the Sisters of Charity so beautifully demonstrate, we should be *prayerful* activists. Prayer connects us with the people and situations around the world for whom and for which we are praying. It reminds us of our motivation: to see the kingdom of God manifest in our world. It reminds us that there is a strong spiritual dimension to all that we do. Above all, prayer reminds us that we cannot do everything by ourselves or in our own power. Ultimately we depend on God to bring his redeeming power to bear in the situations in which we work. Prayer also causes us to stop and take time for reflection. Activists are not action-junkies and taking time to rest is a thoroughly biblical thing to do.(1)

Secondly, we should be *knowledgeable* activists. The problems that face our world are immensely complicated and we must not be simplistic or naïve. Books, magazines, websites, TV and radio programmes will all provide helpful information. One of the best things we can do is join an organization that can give us the resources we need.

Thirdly, we should be *gracious* activists. As I have discovered, it can be easy to become self-righteous and moralistic, preaching to others about where *their* lifestyle is wrong. Jesus made it clear that we must focus on our own failures first

(Matthew 7:3–5). It may take all our lives to remove the plank in our own eyes before we can remove the speck from someone else's!

Being activists is what this book is about. The following chapters aim to give us knowledge and a way forward along this route.

Action points

- Find out about the organizations listed at www.lisforlifestyle.com. Check out their websites and begin to build up your knowledge of some of the issues we shall be looking at in further chapters.
- As you do so, ask God to give you vision and fill you with Jesus' compassion.

Endnote

1 CAFOD, Christian Aid and Tearfund all produce helpful prayer material that can help our prayers maintain a global focus.

B IS FOR BANANAS

My eldest daughter loves bananas, and her grandma often tells her that one day she will end up looking like one. Indeed bananas have become one of the basic foods that we all eat today: so basic that the banana is the world's most popular fruit, worth £5 billion a year, and in the UK 95% of households buy them. We eat more bananas than we do apples; they are the most valuable food product in supermarkets, outsold only by petrol and lottery tickets.

Yet my parents' generation almost never ate them. Do we ever stop to think what has taken place in order for bananas to be such an ordinary part of our lives, rather than an exotic fruit that we rarely see? As commonplace as they may seem, bananas are the perfect way to introduce us to the big, complex game that is global trade.

This is the story of the Banana War. Traditionally, Britain bought her bananas from her former colonies, particularly the Windward Islands in the Caribbean. Britain invested in the original plantations, and Geest, the company that bought and sold most of the bananas until 1995, is a British company. The Lomé Convention in 1975 formalised the EU's commitment to continue to import bananas from the Windward Islands. This commitment was crucial, since the Windward Islands are almost totally reliant on their banana industry and are able to charge a better price for their bananas than producers elsewhere.

Nearly seventy per cent of the bananas involved in international trade, however, are controlled by the big three American companies: Chiquita, Dole and Del Monte. Not liking the EU protectionist policy on bananas, America complained to the World Trade Organization (WTO), which ruled in favour of the USA. When the EU refused to back down, the US struck back and imposed import tariffs, in the end worth $191.4 million, on EU exports (hitting companies such as Arran Aromatics in Scotland, which found 40% of its turnover affected). It might come as no surprise that the American complaint to the WTO came just days after Chiquita donated $500,000 to the Democratic Party, and that the tariffs were enforced by the Republican-controlled Congress after Chiquita donated $350,000 to them. At the time of writing, the banana wars continue in the WTO, although the quotas protecting Caribbean and African bananas have been removed, making competition even more difficult for the small producers.

Despite the growth of fairtrade bananas in Britain, the overwhelming majority of the bananas that we consume both in the UK and in the US are produced in bad conditions. There are two main issues here. First, the plantation workers live in poverty. In Nicaragua, for example, the workers are paid just $1.30 a day, and some independent producers in Ecuador get 3p per pound (450 g), which does not cover costs.

On average, the non-fairtrade producer gets only 5% of the price of a banana; as with many other commodities exported to the north, nearly 90% of the price stays in the north (much with the supermarkets) and is never seen by the producer.

Secondly, vast quantities of chemicals are used to treat the bananas during their production. Plantations in Central America apply 40 kg of active ingredients per hectare per year, more than ten times the average for intensive farming in industrialized countries. In Costa Rica, most banana workers suffer health damage, such as skin lesions or respiratory problems, whilst tens of thousands of male workers across banana-exporting countries are sterile due to one of the toxic pesticides. In Ecuador, entire communities suffer from indiscriminate aerial crop-spraying.

The impact on the environment need hardly be stated, let alone the fact that massive deforestation has taken place to provide the land for the plantations. The effect of all these chemicals on those of us who eat them is something we shall consider in a later chapter. It is interesting to note, however, the response of a banana worker on a Chiquita plantation in Guatemala, on being asked if he ever ate the bananas he produced: '*Good Lord, no! . . . People in places like this don't eat the fruit they cut. I guess we know better.*'

Although we are focusing on bananas, it is no surprise to learn that many other foods are also produced and traded in ways that do great damage to the producers, such as chocolate, tea, sugar and rice, and also goods such as clothes, electronic goods and children's toys. One commodity that is little known about is jewellery, something about which I have gained some understanding since my husband opened an ethical jewellery shop in 2000! It has been an eye-opening journey as we have discovered the horrors that lie behind this industry. On average, for every 10 grams of gold that reaches the shops, 3 tonnes of toxic waste (cyanide or mercury) are created and often washed into the rivers that local people depend on for their fresh water. 100 million people are dependent upon small-scale mining globally, making it the second biggest employer in the world after agriculture and textiles, and a massively important area in which to be working to bring about positive change (see www.credjewellery.com and www.communitymining.org).

It is a harsh reality that we are able to buy the things we do, at the prices we enjoy, because those who are making or producing them are not being paid a proper wage by the large companies that own them.

But are there alternatives, and is there anything that we can do about it?

The answer is 'yes' to both questions. There are three routes open to us. The first is *Fair trade*. Fairtrade (FT) schemes cut out the middlemen and work directly with cooperatives and farmers' associations that are organised and governed so that they are accountable to their members. They guarantee a fixed minimum price that covers the cost of sustainable production, providing a floor price that helps protect small holders against fluctuations in commodity prices. On top of this there is a premium of between 10 – 15% (depending on the product) that is invested by the producer organisations into priority projects such as schools and health centres and business development. The fairtrade scheme means that there is a commitment on the part of the traders to engage in long-term trading relationships which provide greater income security, and so helps the producers to invest in the future. In addition to this, traders commit to making finance available at market rates so that producer organisations can meet the demands of the contract, such as investment in seeds or tools etc.

Since first writing this book, fairtrade has exploded in the UK, with retail sales increasing from £32.9 million in 2000 to £290 million in 2006. In 1996, 2,500 of the world's 10 million sold bananas were fairtrade and none were available in the UK. In 2007, fairtrade bananas made up 30% of the UK banana market, a figure boosted considerably by Sainsbury's decision in that year to convert its entire banana range to fairtrade. Fairtrade tea and coffee are now widely available in coffee shops, both on the high street and on the station platform, and M&S now sell only fairtrade tea and coffee. Worldwide, consumers spent £1.1 bn on fairtrade certified products in 2006: a 42% increase from 2005.

If ever there is a case of consumer power, it is here, and I hope that the story of fairtrade's success in the UK will encourage and motivate those of you who are from other countries! I remember badgering Tesco constantly over its refusal to stock fairtrade bananas when other supermarkets were introducing them. We emailed back and forth for ages until eventually they told me that they would not be stocking fairtrade bananas and that was the end of it: they would not reply to any more of my emails! And yet now they have given in to consumer pressure and do in fact sell fairtrade bananas. Similarly with fairtrade coffee. It may be coincidence, but perhaps Sainsbury's decision to stock large jars of Café Direct had something to do with me constantly asking them to do so.

FT succeeds when the whole supply chain can be controlled, and hence works best with foodstuffs, but also with cotton clothing. FT is the ideal that must be striven for. The present reality, though, is that few companies can truthfully assert that they know how all their goods are produced, since a typical supply chain is vast. (Sainsbury's, for example, estimates that it takes the produce of a million farms around the globe.)

With this in mind, the second alternative route available to us, where FT is not yet an option, is to push for *ethical trade*. Ethical trade is about ensuring that minimum international labour standards are met. These standards include freely chosen employment; freedom to form trade unions; safe and hygienic working conditions; no child labour; payment of living wages; no excessive working hours; minimum environmental damage and no discrimination. For this to happen, companies need to be prepared to aim for longer-term solutions, improving supply chains through incremental changes. Most of the goods we buy will not carry a FT label, but we can still play our part in encouraging companies to operate more ethically by becoming more educated and informed about the products we are purchasing, and asking questions of the companies whenever we want to buy from them.

Chocolate is a good example. Fairtrade chocolate is now a familiar item on British supermarket shelves and counters, but when I first wrote this book it wasn't available (the first fairtrade chocolate bar – Maya Gold – was launched one month after this book was published, which shows just how much has changed!). Alongside the fairtrade movement, however, there has also been a lot of other work that has gone into improving the situation, thanks to the work of organisations such as the World Cocoa Foundation (www.worldcocoafoundation.org) and the International Cocoa Initiative (www.cocoainitiative.org). When you consider that only just over 1% of chocolate sold in the UK is fairtrade, it is clear that the cocoa industry still faces immense problems. However, by supporting the work that these organisations do, and making our own views known to the major brands, we can help move things in the right direction.

The third route is *trade justice*. One of the main ways a country can be lifted out of its poverty is through increasing its exports to the richer countries. The rules for international trade, however, are governed by the commercial and financial interests of those richer countries and thus are shaped to their own advantage. These rules are enforced primarily through three institutions: the WTO, the International Monetary Fund and the World Bank.(1) Trade justice is about seeing a major overhaul happen to the current system so that the rules work *for* poor people rather than against them. This reform of the institutions would include measures like making poverty eradication a key objective, ensuring a truly democratic and transparent process and monitoring the activities of transnational corporations as well as of governments. As citizens and consumers we can be using our voices to call for these changes to take place.(2)

With so many avenues open to us, we can begin playing our part in changing, for the good, the lives of the people who grow or make the things we buy. We have already seen how Jesus' parable of the Good Samaritan teaches us that we are to be neighbours to those whom others ignore, and this applies to those living next door and those on the other side of the world. Through taking the time and trouble to buy fairly-traded products, and by getting involved in working for a fairer and more ethical trading system, we can take a step towards being that neighbour ourselves.

Action points

- Increase your awareness of the issues behind the products you buy. Take time to ask retailers where the product comes from and whether they have looked into the conditions of the producers. For more information on food and supermarkets, see 'F is for Food'.
- If there is a fairtrade option for the product you are buying, buy it! This will often mean shopping

somewhere other than the supermarket and being prepared to pay a higher price. If you find this hard to swallow, tell yourself that you are paying the price you should be paying anyway and are stopping others getting ripped off.

- Consider setting up a Traidcraft stall at your place of work or worship. That way, you and others can gain access to a greater number of fairly traded goods than the supermarkets provide.
- Find out more about the Trade Justice Movement and consider how you might get involved.

Endnotes

1 There is not the space here to look in detail at how these-organizations are set up and run. For more information, see J. Stiglitz, *Globalization and Its Discontents*, and the excellent resources that can be obtained from the World Development Movement, Oxfam and Christian Aid. See also the relevant websites: www.wto.org; www.imf.org; www.worldbank.org.

2 The Trade Justice Movement gives us the opportunity to do exactly that. It is a coalition of organizations campaigning to see these changes take place so that trade works for everyone. It brings together aid agencies, environment and human-rights campaigns, FT organizations and faith and consumer groups. For more information, see www.tradejusticemovement.org.uk.

C IS FOR CREATION

I am pleased that C comes so near the beginning of the alphabet and that creation can be one of the first things we consider, because it is such a vitally important subject. Certainly, those outside the church seem to recognize this: governments and businesses are keen to show their environmental credentials, and any conference worth its salt will feature the environment on its agenda somewhere. Yet the sad fact is that, somehow, the church has not viewed it as such a priority and that is strange because, while others may talk about the environment, we are talking about *creation*.

Christians believe in a trinitarian God – Father, Son and Holy Spirit – who made the universe and the world that we live in and who has declared that it is 'very good' (Genesis 1:31). Some theologies have promoted muddled notions of a separation between body and spirit, earth and heaven, natural and spiritual, exalting the latter and denigrating the former, so that nature/creation is thought to be inferior to the 'supernatural' realm. In contrast to this, the world carries within it the intrinsic value of something that God has made and finds pleasure in – and note that God pronounced creation 'good' before humanity was created. Because he has made it, it belongs to him, first and foremost, and to humanity only secondly (Psalm 24:1). While we are appointed to govern on his behalf (Genesis 1:26–30), it is only through his continual influence that the Earth is sustained. One of the key biblical principles arising out of this is that the right of all to use the Earth's resources comes before anyone's right to ownership. The Earth, then, has been given to us not as something that God no longer cares about, but as a gift that we are to treasure and look after.

In the Old Testament, the idea of dominion is used of the Hebrew kings and embodies within it the idea of 'servant kingship', reflecting God's own kingly rule within creation, which is undoubtedly a caring and providing one rather than one of domination. Genesis 1:26–28, however, has caused problems in the church through a misunderstanding of the words 'dominion' and 'subdue', and hence a misunderstanding of the account of creation as a whole. This has led some to an anthropocentric view of creation that holds that everything revolves around humanity and was made for our benefit. It is certainly true that there is a distinction between human beings and the rest of creation: we are the only ones to have been made 'in the image of God' and to have been set apart to have dominion over the rest of creation. This can be seen in Adam's naming of the animals – a significant act in the Bible (and it is interesting to note that the Muslim account of creation has God, not Adam, giving the animals their names). Because of this distinction between humanity and the rest of creation, the psalmist can describe humanity as being a little lower than the heavenly beings (or God) and crowned with glory and splendour, and as having the rest of God's creation 'under their feet' (Psalm 8:5–6).

That distinction between humanity and the rest of creation, though, needs to be held in tension with the reality that we are also a part of creation and not superior to it. It is an inescapable fact that we are part of the same ecosystems and structures that form the rest of creation. In fact, as the Old Testament scholar, Dr. Chris Wright states, the opening chapters of Genesis 'do not immediately emphasize human uniqueness. On the contrary, it seems that at point after point we have more in common with the rest of the animate creation than in distinction from it.' We might even question the popular interpretation that sees humanity as the climax of creation, since a less human-centred approach would see the real consummation and goal of creation as God's rest on day seven, which reminds us that all creation exists for God, to worship him, rather than for humanity.

Of immense significance in the creation narrative is the description of humanity as being made 'in God's image'. We began to explore what this phrase means in 'A is for Activists'. One meaning that the author of Genesis particularly highlights is to do with the role that we are given regarding the rest of creation. Indeed, Chris Wright makes the point that the grammar used in Genesis 1:26–28 indicates that this is one of the main reasons why humanity is so made: 'because God intended this last-created species, the human species, to exercise dominion over the rest of his creatures, for that reason God expressly and purposefully creates this species alone in his own image'. The sense of the verses could then be read as, 'Let us make human beings in our own image and likeness, *so that* they may exercise dominion over the rest of creation'.

'The image of God' carries the idea of being God's representative on earth in the same way that physical images of a king would be set up throughout his territory to signal his lordship. By being made in his image, God has given us delegated authority over his creation. It should go without saying that we exercise that authority in a way that reflects his character, not through brutality and carelessness, but with love and compassion and service. Once I had understood the meaning of 'the image of God' in this way, it transformed my outlook. Suddenly I realised that one of the main reasons why I am here is to look after the rest of what God has made. That was, and still is, very exciting and also very humbling.

Our representation of the image of God, however, has been marred by the fall because humanity turned away from God and people chose to go their own way. The fall broke humanity's relationship with God, with other humans, and with the rest of creation, which would now carry within itself the curse of God as well as his blessing. The rest of the Bible tells the story of the unfolding plan of God for salvation. Israel is called to be his people and model his purposes for servant kingship, and there is a particular relationship with the land that acts as a spiritual barometer of her obedience (e.g. Deuteronomy 30:15–16; Isaiah 5:8–10; Jeremiah 5:23–25).

Our relationship with the rest of creation finds its centre in the coming of Jesus to live on earth as a human being, to die and be raised to life again. God's plan finds its fulfilment in Jesus, who affirms creation by choosing to become a part of that creation and, by dying and being raised to life again and ascending into heaven with his resurrected body, brings potential healing to every broken relationship (2 Corinthians 5:18–21; Ephesians 2:11–18; Romans 8:19–22). It is crucial to understand that God's intention for salvation involves the whole of creation, not just humanity alone (see also Colossians 1:15–20).

Revelation 4 is a stunning vision of the whole of creation,

including human beings, worshipping the Lord God Almighty. This is the end for which we have been made: to worship God completely and to enable the rest of creation to be made perfect in order to praise its Creator. This is a great privilege, but also an awesome responsibility. As Colin Gunton said, 'We human creatures are the centre of the world's problems, and only by our redirection will the whole creation be set free'. Here therefore we see that, if evangelism and social transformation are to be truly reflecting God's mission, we must also be involved in ecological care.

The Bible ends with a wonderful picture of the new heaven and the new earth (Revelation 21 – 22). This picture describes how the world that God has made as the new Jerusalem comes down from heaven – we do not 'go up there'. All things are made new in Jesus, involving all of creation, as the tree of life bears its fruit for all humanity to enjoy and the curse of the fall is finally ended. In a manner similar to our own resurrected bodies, there is both discontinuity (seen in 2 Peter 3:3–16) and continuity (seen in Romans 8:18–30) between the present and the new heaven and earth.[(1)] The emphasis of the word 'new' is on transformation rather than destruction, indicating 'newness in terms of quality rather than of something new that has never been in existence'. In this way, we understand 'the new creation itself not as a replacement for the present world but as the eschatological [relating to end times] future of this world'.

This spurs us on to action. In 'A is for Activists' we saw how our future hope gives us the motivation for how we live today, in active expectancy and anticipation. Just as the incentive for our lives is to be seeing God's kingdom brought into this world now, so too, no less, with the rest of creation: it is our future hope that inspires us to work for its present, albeit partial, realization. This, for me, is what gives me my motivation for life and for doing the things that I do: I want to live my life in such a way that I am building into that eschatological future when the whole of creation will be able to praise its maker fully, rather than doing things that work against that.

What does that mean for us?

First, we need to be learning about the major threats to God's creation. These are issues such as climate change, deforestation, the loss of species and biodiversity, consumer waste and pollution. We shall be exploring all of these things further in later chapters.

Secondly, we can then begin to consider what we can do in our own lives to start making a difference. When looking at such huge problems, it can be helpful to see ourselves standing within concentric circles, each circle representing a wider area for involvement. These areas are: ourselves, our church, our local community, our country and our world.

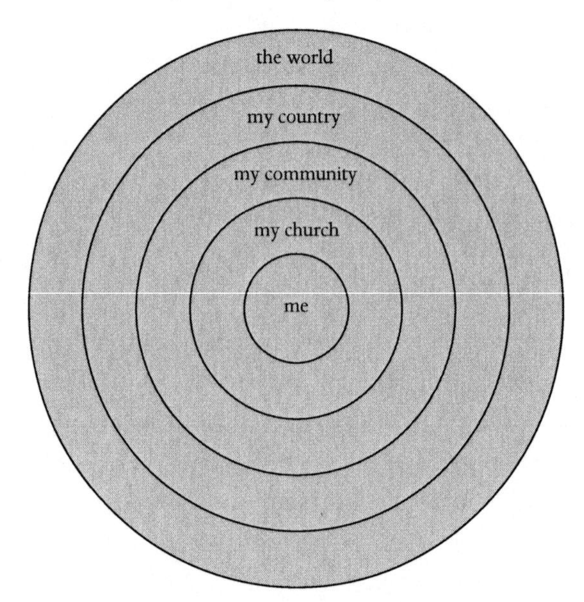

So, for example, we can change some of the everyday things we do, perhaps increasing what we recycle or reducing our car usage. In our churches, maybe we could consider carrying out an environmental audit (Eco-congregation can help with this, see their details at www.lisforlifestyle.com) or, again, simply encourage people to walk or cycle to church. In our local communities, there may be a conservation organization or Local Agenda 21 programme that we could join. Perhaps we could encourage our local authorities to improve recycling facilities. When we move on to our country and world, we begin to enter the area of campaigning and letter-writing. Here it is useful to belong to a national or international organization that will help us in this. We shall look more closely at a lot of these things in later chapters.

What we have to remember is that we cannot do everything. But that is no reason to do nothing! While each little action we take *is* only a drop in the ocean, those drops will make a difference. Not only is this our responsibility, it is a part of the essence of being people created by God that we care for the rest of what he has created.

Action points

- Increase your awareness and understanding of the created world in which you live. Stop to smell a flower, notice a particular colour, watch a bird fly, follow the seasons in your garden . . .
- Find out about the organizations listed on the website and, if financially able, join the one that you think will help you the most.

Endnote

1 This is of course based on the 'first fruits' of Jesus' resurrection body, which demonstrates both continuity and discontinuity with his old body and is both physical and spiritual as he eats fish yet walks through walls.

D IS FOR DRIVING

We've all seen the advertisements on the TV: just you, in your car, driving along an empty road. To drive a car is the stuff that life is made of. You are in control; you have the money and the look; you have the power to make your life whatever you want it to be. In a world of confusion and instability, your car is the one thing you can rely on: a safe haven from life's storms. Your car is, indeed, a car to be proud of.

There is no doubt that the car has brought many benefits. It is convenient to hop into the car and nip to the shops. In winter it is more comfortable and, in our busy lives, driving saves so much time. It increases our employment options, allowing us to take a job some distance away, and helps us keep in touch with our scattered family and friends.

It is amazing to think how, over the course of just a few decades, our lifestyles have become so dependent on the car. There are somewhere between 500–600 million cars in the world and nearly 29 million new cars are made each year. Of those 480 million, 90% are owned by the sixteen wealthiest countries (one fifth of the world's population). In the UK the car is used for more and more shorter journeys. Twenty-five per cent of car trips are under two miles long and 61% are under five miles. In the USA in 2005 1,689,965,000,000 miles were driven by passenger cars! Motor vehicles now produce nearly a quarter of America's CO_2 emissions.

As we look at these statistics, it does not take much imagination to realise that, whatever the benefits, our car-dependent culture is also bringing great costs. The first cost is to ourselves. The emissions from a car consist of carbon monoxide, carbon dioxide, lead, nitrogen dioxide, benzene, hydrocarbons and particulates. None of these is good for our health! Indeed, benzene is a known cancer-causing chemical, and it is no coincidence that the number of asthma cases has doubled in the UK in the last fifteen years. Road traffic is the fastest-growing source of air pollution and constitutes 70% of carbon monoxide emissions. Interestingly, tests show that, in heavy traffic, pollution levels are higher inside a car than outside it. In contrast to the health problems caused by driving, a regular adult cyclist shows the fitness level of a person ten years younger than a non-cyclist of the same age.

The problem is even worse in other parts of the world. *The Times of India* states that breathing the air in Mumbai and Delhi is the equivalent of smoking twenty cigarettes a day. In Mexico, the situation is so serious that everybody is banned from driving their cars one day a week, each car being identified by a number on the number plate.

In addition, the increase in car usage has had a dramatic impact on our communities. Parents are afraid to let their children walk to school or play outside because of the traffic. This is understandable when you consider that the most common cause of death for children under fifteen is through road accidents. A transport survey in West Sussex found that 70% of children lived within half a mile of their school, but 45% were regularly driven. Of those 45%, 30% of parents said they would walk or cycle if road safety improvements were made.

It is interesting, too, that car ownership is one of the main indicators of the increasing inequality that is found in the UK. About a quarter of households do not have a car, yet town planning and design favours those with cars, with its emphasis on out-of-town shopping centres. (Interestingly, when I first wrote this book, the figure was a third). People without cars are forced to shop in the smaller, local shops where goods are more expensive. We have seen already how the Old Testament laws such as the Jubilee sought to limit the inequalities that existed between people. For Christians, the improvement of access for all is an issue of equality and justice and we should seize any opportunity to campaign for better-quality public transport and for policies that keep our town centres vibrant.

The second cost is to the environment. We shall look at climate change later, but it is relevant to note here that cars produce a fifth of the UK's carbon dioxide emissions and it is expected that fuel consumption from private-car owners will increase globally by up to 130% in twenty-five years. In the US, motor vehicles produce nearly a quarter of CO_2 emissions.

The effect that road-building has on the countryside was highlighted dramatically by the protests around the building of the M3 through the wetland meadows and chalk grasslands of Twyford Down, and the building of the Newbury Bypass through the precious heathland of Snelsmore Common. Road-building threatens priceless wildlife sites and kills millions of animals. Our petrol comes from the oil that is imported into Britain on sea tankers. There have been several well-publicized and horrific oil disasters, not least that of the *Sea Empress*, which ran aground off Wales in 1996 and spilled 70,000 tonnes of crude oil, ruining the local fishing industry and destroying countless numbers of wildlife and seabirds.

Does it have to be like this? The answer, of course, is no, and there are some inspiring examples of places and people who do things differently. There is a European network of 'car-free cities' that work on the idea that quality of life is greatly improved by not having to provide for cars. Such places are not absolutely car-less, but operate car-sharing schemes. These schemes have reduced the members' mileage by 50% and increased their use of public transport. In Bremen, for example, each shared car is thought to have replaced five private cars.

Working for A Rocha, I now regularly meet people who have either given up using a car altogether or have switched to an electric one. Meet Graham McCaul:

I'm an A Rocha supporter in Sheffield and a local GP. Recently I've taken delivery of an all electric G-wizz car – the first in the city. Made in India, it can be charged up at home or work by an ordinary three pin socket. It does 40 miles on a charge, – or 39 if you listen to the CD player! Maximum speed is 45mph [it is worth pointing out that G-wizz cars now go up to 50!]. *The car uses only a quarter of the energy of the average car, virtually nothing when stood still in a traffic jam, and even charges up when you brake. As we're signed up with a 100% renewable electricity company, this avoids harmful* CO_2 *emissions.*

But what about the majority of us who perhaps aren't courageous enough to make such a change or aren't in a situation where it would be feasible? Is there anything we can do to make a difference?

The obvious answer, of course, is that we must all reduce our dependency on our cars and cut down the amount of times that we use them. *There is no other way round it*; we have to start walking or cycling for those shorter journeys, and using public transport or hiring a car for the longer ones, even if we have a large family. It is an amazing fact that there are an estimated 22 million bikes in the UK, with only 5 million regularly being used. The average person in the UK makes just 14 trips a year by bicycle: a figure that astounds me since I do half that number in a week!

A lot of this is about changing our attitudes. In the US and in the UK we have got so used to driving short distances that the thought of walking or cycling is not a pleasant one; it is so much more *convenient* to drive. We are cocooned in a culture that sees inconvenience as one of the greatest evils, to be avoided at all costs, and so we confuse what we perceive to be a need with what is actually just a nuisance: 'It takes more trouble to cycle or walk, therefore I need to drive.' My mum used to cycle eight miles to school and back every day, even in the rain or the snow. That was nothing amazing – it was just what you did. I sometimes think of that if I am feeling that I would rather drive the 1.5 miles to the leisure centre!

What I have found is that what begins as a discipline ends up becoming a pleasure. I now love to walk or cycle. I love the fact that I am outside, that I am not damaging God's creation in any way. I love the fact that I am getting some exercise; that it gives me space to pray; that I am more aware of what the seasons are doing; that I can appreciate the flowers in people's gardens and the birds in the hedges; that I can say hello to people from my neighbourhood and stop for a chat. I love the fact that my daughters are growing up without the impression that all journeys have to be made in a car (although I have to own up to the fact that, given the choice, they would choose the car any day, much to my chagrin!).

Realistically though, many of us will want to own and use a car, and there are still many things we can do here to make a difference. Always look for ways to car-share: if you know of someone else going to the same place as you, phone them up and offer them a lift. When driving, keep your speed down. Driving at 50 mph uses 25–30% less fuel than driving at 70. I have had to do this gradually. I used to drive regularly at 80 mph (and felt virtuous for keeping my speed down to that!). When I began learning about the environmental costs, I decided to slow down. To jump from 80 mph to 60 is painfully frustrating, so I weaned myself off, five miles at a time: driving at 75 mph until that felt normal, then down to 70 and so on until now I leave home a bit early and drive at 55 to 60, even on long journeys. Yes, it is aggravatingly slow, but you do get used to it and the benefits to the environment and to your purse are worth it! Alongside that, being aware of the road ahead and braking or accelerating gently reduces your fuel consumption significantly.

Keeping your car in good condition improves efficiency. If your car was built before 1993, fit a catalytic converter. Do remember, though, that these only kick in after two miles. Look into having an emissions-saving device fitted. These can reduce emissions by 40% and save at least 10% on fuel costs. Next time you buy a car, choose one that is highly efficient or buy a hybrid car (running on both petrol and electricity) or an electric one.

Finally, we must make sure that we do not fall into the trap of thinking that, if we are being more environmentally sensitive with our cars, it is OK to drive them more! Every time a car is started up, the world God made is damaged in some way. Sadly, every little trip to the supermarket contributes to global warming. As we saw in the previous chapter, the way we treat our world is a fundamental part of what it means to be a Christian. Someone once said to me that to be a disciple of Jesus and knowingly to harm his creation is a contradiction in terms. That is a sobering thought in relation to the amount we drive. So let's drive in a way that does the least damage as possible, and, whenever we can, leave that car at home!

Action points

- Stop using your car for all short distances (and be prepared to lengthen your idea of a short distance!).
- If you have a bicycle, get it serviced so that is in good condition.
- Begin to drive more slowly.
- Do a 'car-fast' for a week and see what happens.

E IS FOR ENERGY

The first thing I did this morning was wake up and have a shower. The water was hot and the house warm, thanks to our gas central heating. I then made Greg and myself cups of tea and warmed our daughters' milk in the microwave. We sat in bed and watched the news on TV and then went downstairs for breakfast: toast made in the toaster and cereal with milk kept cold in the fridge. The children are now at school, no doubt with their cardigans off because the classrooms are over-heated, and I am sitting here writing this, listening to the radio.

Nearly all of those things required energy in the form of gas, petrol or electricity. I have done nothing out of the ordinary, but already I have used a good amount of energy (and not just that required to get me out of bed and the children to school!). Even the water I am drinking has been through an energy-intensive process to rid it, among other things, of the chemicals put in it by industry and agriculture and from the cleaning products we use. The society we have created is totally dependent on using large amounts of energy in order to survive.

Nearly three-quarters of the energy that is used globally comes from fossil fuels (oil, coal and gas) and the rest is from nuclear, hydro and biomass. In the UK, nearly 90% of energy is from fossil fuels and the USA is not much better at 85%. The problems associated with them are colossal.

At the forefront is climate change. I wrote in the Introduction that I hardly need to explain what it is any more. It is sobering, though, to be reminded again of its consequences. As temperatures rise, so will sea levels, although no one is able to predict exactly by how much because there are so many variables. If the Greenland ice cap melts (which is more than likely), sea level will eventually rise by 7metres. Even if that doesn't happen, and even if CO_2 emissions were stopped completely tomorrow, we are already inexorably set on a course of global warming that will cause more frequent and extreme weather events leading to more intense floods and droughts, as well as increased food shortages and disease; millions of environmental refugees; millions of species lost, and a situation in which the poorest people and nations will be most affected.

Forgotten under the urgency of climate change, is acid rain. This is caused by the mixing of water in the atmosphere with nitrogen and sulphur oxides, forming sulphuric acid and nitric acid. These are still causing damage to lakes and forests.

Another very real problem is the depletion of the natural resources that we are using: it is estimated that the amount of oil used globally in a year takes one million years to be formed.

Oil is the key to all of this as it is essential to agriculture, petrochemicals and electricity. Its extraction causes environmental degradation, and this only looks set to worsen as new reserves become harder to find and are opened in such fragile and beautiful places as Alaska, officially a national wildlife refuge.

Because of its central place in the global economy, oil ('black gold') is a major factor in world politics. As leading ethicist Professor Michael Northcott states, 'There is a very clear association between oil extraction, violent conflict and war'. The first Gulf War was waged mainly because of the West's need to access Kuwait's oil. A highly publicized case is Nigeria, where Shell and other companies are involved in oil extraction in Ogoniland. Protests from the Ogoni people that their land has been ruined and their livelihoods destroyed have been met with violence from the Nigerian government. Since 1993, the Nigerian internal security forces have killed over a thousand Ogonis.(1) Oil now accounts for 80% of Nigeria's GDP and 90% of Government revenues, yet the industry employs only 2% of all Nigerians, and deep corruption means that the nation as a whole does not feel the benefit of the oil money.

This way of operating runs strongly against God's intention for his creation. There are two further points to make.

The first is to underline that our environmental crisis is, at its heart, a spiritual issue, linked with humanity's sin. Jon Sobrino has said that 'the question of the poor . . . is fundamentally the question of God, and of what kind of God we worship'. Likewise, how do we regard what God has created? Idolatry is central to our world, in which the false gods of wealth, power and security are worshipped in the place of the one true God. The environmental problems associated with our current use of energy can be attributed to human greed and selfishness; to our consumer society, which expects an ever-increasing standard of living, and to the unrestricted growth of the rich nations. Just one British power station (Drax B in Yorkshire) emits more CO_2 into the atmosphere than the combined carbon emissions of Kenya, Malawi, Mozambique, Tanzania, Uganda and Zambia. In addition, the average American consumes twice as much energy as the average Briton.

This link between the misuse of the land and human sin is clearly seen in the Old Testament prophets. Hosea 4:1b–3 provides a good example:

> *'There is no faithfulness, no love,*
> *no acknowledgment of God in the land . . .*
> *Because of this the land mourns,*
> *and all who live in it waste away;*
> *the beasts of the field and the birds of the air*
> *and the fish of the sea are dying'.*

Secondly, species extinction, which is occurring at a rate 98% higher than is natural, brings a spiritual challenge. Romans 1:20 makes it clear that creation reveals the character of God, as does Psalm 104 and Job 38–42. The story of Noah demonstrates God's saving and loving care for all living things: the purpose of including two of every living thing in the ark was 'to keep their various kinds alive throughout the earth' (Genesis 7:3). From this perspective, John Stott is right to say that 'extinction is blasphemy'; and Metropolitan Archbishop Daniel of Moldova makes the sad point that 'extinction is a loss of our knowledge of God – erasing his fingerprints'.

Our use of energy reflects our inability to imagine living any other way. However, our societies must wean themselves off the dependency on fossil fuels. Some cite nuclear power as an alternative, which already supplies the US with 8.2% of its energy and the UK with 4%. Primarily, this is because it has very low carbon dioxide emissions. Safety scares, the real cost of nuclear power (subsidized by £1 billion a year in the 1990s in the UK) and the lack of solution to the problem of nuclear waste, however, give it distinct drawbacks. Some feel that, at least in the short term, nuclear energy may be necessary if we are to cut our emissions to the necessary level. But the debate continues.

The alternative has to come from renewable energy: from wind, water, tides, waves, biomass and solar energy (Spencer and White's, *Christianity, Climate Change and Sustainable Living*, give an excellent overview of the different alternatives and their pros and cons). At the moment, only 2.8% of electricity in the UK and 6.8% in the US comes from a renewable source. For this to increase, our governments must be prepared to put the necessary investment into developing these services.

So what are the areas in which we can begin to play our part? First, since transport is the fastest-growing source of carbon dioxide emissions and accounts for 34% of an average American's, and 29% of a British resident's emissions, everything that we looked at in our last chapter applies here too: reduce car usage. Of course, cars are not the only issue: the environmental costs of both flying and food transportation must be considered. Both we will look at these later in this book.

Secondly, since 25% of the UK's carbon dioxide emissions comes from our houses, much energy saving is possible. We can use low-energy light-bulbs (saving 80%); fit a SAVA plug on to our fridges and freezers; insulate our homes effectively, and wash our clothes on cooler temperatures with full loads. And interestingly, the production of 'disposable' nappies uses far more energy than the washing of washable ones. We should turn all appliances off standby: the energy used to keep all our TVs on standby would power a medium-sized town like Basingstoke, in the UK. Similarly, if everyone boiled just the amount of water that was needed in the kettle instead of filling it up, enough energy would be saved to power the whole of the UK's streetlights for the following night. Most importantly, we can reduce the amount of energy we use for heating and hot water. Turning the thermostat down by just 1°C or using one hour less heating a day can save 10% on fuel bills, while showering uses a quarter of the water of a bath (further ideas can be found in Tearfund's action paper on *Climate Change*). As we do these things we shall reduce our energy bills, demonstrating that self-interest and global responsibility can go hand in hand.

Thirdly, we can actively promote the use of renewable energy by switching to a 'green' electricity supplier (such as Good Energy or Ecotricity) or going on to a 'green' tariff with our existing supplier (ScottishPower, Powergen and Southern Electricity are the best). The current situation in the UK is quite complicated, with controversy over the Renewable Obligation system, which was designed to stimulate the UK market for renewable energy, but many feel that it is not doing the job (see the Energy Saving Trust or the National Energy Foundation, details on www.lisforlifestyle.com). Some conservation organizations (such as the Royal Society for the Protection of Birds) have their own schemes affiliated to 'green' suppliers, and by switching to these we can go 'green', simultaneously supporting our chosen organization.

Fourthly, we can reduce the amount of meat that we eat. This might come as a surprise, but we shall see in the next chapter that, globally, meat and dairy production contributes more to climate change than the entire global transport sector combined. We must not ignore the implications that this has for our predominantly meat-based diets.

Finally, we can ask our MPs to put pressure on the government to provide more support for renewable energy and energy efficiency; to create policies that will reduce the UK's carbon dioxide emissions, and to play its part in persuading other countries to act similarly.

Action points

- Decide on five ways in which you will reduce the amount of energy you use around the home. When you are doing these five easily, choose another five. If you live with your family, try to include them by asking them to imagine ways of reducing energy.
- Buy your electricity from a green supplier (Ecotricity and Good Energy are the best options).
- Get involved in the Stop Climate Chaos coalition.
- Look at the Transition Towns initiative (www.transitiontowns.org).

Endnotes

1 Southern Sudan is another place where people's lives are being ruined because of fighting around oil (for more details contact Christian Aid).
2 Both the books for this chapter are recommended on the lisforlifestyle website.

F IS FOR FOOD

I am obsessed with food. There are no two ways about it: food is the subject that I will talk about most passionately and about which I am becoming frighteningly puritanical! So what has happened to cause this mania in me? I blame it all on the innocent boxes of locally grown organic vegetables that have been coming into our house every week for the last few years.

To begin with, I really disliked the scheme, but did it because I felt I ought to. The vegetables were often dirty, needing a good soak and a scrub, taking up time. I found the seasonal aspect of it frustrating, and I disliked the blemishes and imperfections that the vegetables sometimes had on them.

Over the last few years, however, these same vegetables have taken me on a journey of discovery about the food we eat. I now look at them in a completely new light. These days I love the fact that my food comes with the soil still attached to it. It reminds me that my food does not come from a plastic bag, but from the ground. Scrubbing the soil off my carrots gives me contact with the earth that produced it and reminds me of the labour that went into growing it.

I now love the fact that the vegetables come in seasons. Again, it brings me back into contact with nature, away from the bright lights and plastic bags of the supermarkets. It teaches me that things have their seasons – a very biblical idea – and helps me to appreciate the rhythm that is in life (Ecclesiastes 3:1–8; Psalm 1:3). There is no doubt, too, that many vegetables grown and harvested in season taste far better than the vegetables I used to buy, and so waiting brings a greater appreciation for them.

I have also grown to love my vegetables coming in all different shapes and sizes with their lumps and bumps. I now positively dislike having to buy vegetables in the supermarket: the rows of perfectly shaped and identically sized produce depresses me. How did they get like that, anyway?

One answer is that anything that does not meet the industry or supermarket standards regarding length, size, lack of blemishes and so on is thrown away. The other answer is that vegetables and fruit are produced like that through the use of chemicals: insecticides, herbicides and pesticides. Around 25,000 tonnes of pesticides were applied to UK crops in 2000 and, altogether, 430 different pesticides are permitted for use in non-organic farming (this contrasts with only four pesticides that are allowed under the Soil Association's standards: soft soap, sulphur and copper – which are from traditional use in organic farming – and rotenone, which is of natural origin). For example, Cox apples can sometimes receive 36 different pesticides, through 16 sprayings. Many of these are systemic, which means they permeate into the flesh of the fruit and so cannot be removed through peeling or washing.

While this activity may produce big, perfect-looking vegetables, it is damaging to the environment and to human health. There is growing concern over what has been called the 'cocktail effect': continual exposure to low levels of a variety of different chemicals, which could affect long-term health. As yet, little research has been done into this, so possible dangers are unknown. Because of financial gain, chemicals are often released too early into the market before being properly researched. Some years later, dangers become apparent and they have to be withdrawn. (Lindane is an infamous example). The potential danger of these chemicals to babies and young children is particularly worrying, as their bodies are less able to deal with the toxic effects.

Bringing up children has turned many people, including me, towards organic food.(1) And it seems as if I'm not the only one. Although overall organic food accounts for only 3–4% of total food sales in the UK, and only 2.8% of food sales in the US, there is no doubt that the organic industry is growing rapidly. Since writing this book, I have seen it go from fringe and somewhat weird to mainstream. In both the UK and the US, organic food and drink sales are growing by over 20% each year and 2005–2006 saw direct-sales organic produce (i.e. from box schemes or farmers' markets etc.) grow by a staggering 53%.

The damage being done to the environment and to biodiversity is only too evident when you look at the difference in wildlife on organic and intensive farms. A review showed that on organic farms there were five times as many wild plants in arable fields and 57% more species. Some endangered species on farmland were found only on organic farms. There were 44% more birds in fields outside the breeding season and, again, endangered birds such as the song thrush were significantly more numerous on organic farms. In particular, there were more than twice as many breeding skylarks.

Intensive farming has been happening for only the last fifty years – the post-war period when, understandably, the rationing caused by a loss of food imports led the government to produce a new food policy that would encourage maximum production. The consumer's constant desire for cheap food has encouraged this to continue, so that since the 1950s we have seen a huge increase in production while prices have fallen. The way that our world has developed since then has allowed us to import whatever we want, whenever we want. This has benefited us with cheap food all year round and an endless variety of products.

We are now beginning to realize, however, that cheap food is coming at a heavy cost. Apart from the effects of intensive farming on the environment and on biodiversity, there is also the effect of the transport and packaging involved in much of our food. It is thought that 75% of the cost of food is in its processing, packaging and distribution. We often hear now about the issue of 'food miles' and it is a sobering fact that a quarter of heavy-goods vehicle trips are food-related. With apples, for example, each kilogramme from New Zealand that is imported into the UK produces its own weight in carbon dioxide emissions.

Then there are the implications for our health: we hardly need reminding of salmonella, BSE, Foot and Mouth, Bird Flu and controversial genetically modified (GM) foods.(2) Moving away from the negative, though, there are thought to be positive benefits in eating organic foods. Research carried out since the first edition of this book now shows that no other food has higher amounts of beneficial minerals, essential amino acids and vitamins than organic food. For example, according to research conducted by European scientists, organic milk has nearly 70% more essential fatty acid omega-3 than its non-organic equivalent.

The welfare of farmed animals is also important. Thanks to factory farming, the meat that was most expensive when my parents were children (chicken) and the fish that was most expensive when I was a child (salmon) are now among the cheapest that can be bought. When you look at the conditions in which both are produced, however, you understand why. Instead of describing the life of a battery chicken, let me quote the wonderful chef, Hugh Fearnley-Whittingstall, who says that anyone who buys such meat is 'either an idiot or a heartless bastard'. The same conditions apply to the salmon that is now available, so I try not to eat salmon unless it is from an organic farm or MSC-certified (see further, K is for Kippers).

These issues have become much more well known since I first wrote this book. In 2008, British chefs Hugh Fearnley-Whittingstall and Jamie Oliver were at the fore-front of a highly publicised campaign to stop consumers buying intensively-farmed chickens. So far the campaign seems to be working, as demand has rocketed, but time will only tell if the British consumer will sustain this move. My own little adventures in keeping laying hens and rearing pigs and chickens for meat has only served to heighten my appreciation for these issues (and shown me that there really is a huge difference in the quality of the meat produced). It is crucial that, as Christians, we only use our money to support those who look after the animals that we will eat. After all, as Proverbs says, 'a righteous person cares for the needs of his animal' (12:10).

From a global perspective, we also need to be aware of the consequences of our current high meat consumption. It may be a surprise to some that the report from the UN's Food and

Agricultural Organisation, *Livestock's Long Shadow*, showed that meat and dairy production contributes more to climate change than the entire global transport sector combined (18% versus 13.5%). The report found the livestock industry to be 'one of the top two or three most significant contributors to the most serious environmental problems, at every scale from local to global', contributing to land degradation, climate change, air pollution, water shortage and water pollution and loss of biodiversity.

The vegetarian/vegan/meat-eating debate is a complex and contentious one, not least because it involves the dilemma: 'what relative value should we assign to the environment, compared to other objectives such as the provision of livelihoods or the cheap supply of animal products?'. I cannot look at this debate in depth, but I would encourage all of you to study the questions for yourselves and, at the very least, reduce the amount of meat that you eat.

Alongside all of this is an issue of power. I do not want to create the impression that all farmers are heartless people, intent on destroying the environment. That is wrong. Many farmers care strongly for their animals and for their land, including those who are non-organic.(3) In fact, as has been well documented, farming is in a crisis. In 2004 one dairy farm closed every day. No, the problem lies with those who control what happens in farming: the biotechnology companies who produce the pesticides; the big food manufacturers, who can influence what kind of food is grown; and the supermarkets that control distribution and dictate prices and uniformity of produce. (80% of money spent on food is spent at the supermarkets, 32% of money spent on food is spent at Tesco, and it is well known that one in every eight pounds in the British economy is spent at Tesco.) Pivotal to these is the government, which should be better involved in issues of food labelling, safety standards and supporting good farming practices.

As Wendell Berry says, how and what we eat is a political issue – an issue of freedom.

There is a politics of food that, like any politics, involves our freedom. We still (sometimes) remember that we cannot be free if our minds and voices are controlled by someone else. But we have neglected to understand that we cannot be free if our food and our sources are controlled by someone else. The condition of the passive consumer of food is not a democratic condition. One reason to eat responsibly is to eat free.

Our attitude to food is influenced by other aspects of our lives. The chapter 'S is for Simplicity' shows how our use of time reflects our values and affects many areas of our lives. This is no less true with regards to food. Biblically, food is a part of the gift relationship that God established with humanity in the Garden of Eden. We see there the goodness of food as a gift from God to sustain us. This is reflected in the way we use food as a central part of our relationship-building. Our demand for convenience, as seen already in 'D is for Driving', threatens to erode the relational aspect of food.

There is thus a spiritual side to food. See how often the Bible links food and eating with central biblical concepts (communion, the water of life, fasting, 'taste and see that the LORD is good', the eschatological banquet and so on). Author and Christian environmentalist Michael Schut views food as a sacrament and talks of 'the spirituality embodied in our personal and cultural relationship to food'. I see the food I eat and the way I produce it as one of the ways in which I worship God, eating and producing in a manner that respects what he has created, both human and non-human. As Christians we must do no less.

Action points

- Buy local, organic food, and as little as possible from the supermarket (but see 'Q is for Questions' for a more detailed discussion). Farm shops, delivery boxes and farmers' markets are great ways to do this (the Soil Association provides information on these). Get together with friends to form a food cooperative, enabling you to buy organic and fairtrade food at wholesale prices (see www.infinityfoods.co.uk). If you have to choose, go local rather than organic, but try to do both! Christian Ecology Link has devised a useful mnemonic – just follow the LOAF principle: Local, Organic, Animal-friendly and Fairly-traded (see website).
- Grow (and rear!) your own food. Whether you have an allotment or just a windowsill, you can grow some of your own things, making the connection between your food and the land. You will know exactly what has gone into it and the food miles will be zero.
- Question your supermarket constantly (contact Friends of the Earth's 'Real Food Campaign' for help and see 'B is for Bananas' for more on fairtrade). Let them know what you would like their policies to be ('L is for Letters' looks further at this). If you use different supermarkets compare their answers.
- Shop wisely and only buy what you will eat. 30% of food is currently thrown away by consumers (for more on this see www.wrap.org.uk).

Endnotes

1 I am concentrating on vegetables and fruit here, but the same can, of course, also be said of meat with the little-known dangers of eating animals that have been regularly

given antibiotics and are themselves eating feeds that contain pesticides.

2 I am not going to cover GM foods in this book. For more information contact Friends of the Earth and the Soil Association, and see Humphrys, *The Great Food Gamble*, ch. 8.

3 A positive development in farming is a move towards 'integrated farm management', a system of farming that includes the use of traditional techniques along with modern pesticides and that aims to minimize environmental impact. Their view is that pesticides contribute importantly to our health and quality of life by, for example, enabling crops to be produced more efficiently, reducing the contamination of food by toxic fungi, and controlling insects that spread human diseases. Recognizing their potential dangers, however, their approach is that one should 'use as much pesticide as is necessary to do the job, but as little as possible'. For more details, contact the Crop Protection Association UK at www.cropprotection.org.uk and the British Crop Protection Council at www.bcpc.org. Food produced under this system bears the LEAF marque (Linking Environment and Farming: see www.leafmarque.com).

G IS FOR GLOBALIZATION

'Let's see how many countries we represent today,' I asked the people in my seminar. 'Have a look at the clothes you're wearing, the bag you're carrying, your phone . . . and see where they all come from.' As people called out, it soon became clear that we were wearing and using things from all around the world: jeans from Morocco, a pen from Malaysia, an apple from New Zealand, a bag from Bali, a diary from China . . .

In 'A is for Activists' we looked at what it means to be people who want to spend themselves on behalf of the hungry and satisfy the needs of the oppressed (Isaiah 58:10). If we are to work effectively in our world, we need to understand the context in which our world is set.

This is where the word 'globalization' comes in. There are certain words that sum up the story that people find themselves in, and that give people meaning and a way to understand the world. As Ian Linden puts it, 'Today the word "globalization" encapsulates our latest contemporary story.' The Department for International Development (DFID) provides a good definition of globalization as being simply 'the process by which the world is becoming more and more connected and interdependent'. People's answers in the seminar I was leading on globalization proved the point. In particular, since the events of 11 September 2001, we are realizing how interlinked we are with the rest of our world.

The word 'globalization' generates huge debate between those who are for it and those who are against it. Globalization is bound up with the theory of free-trade market capitalism (that is, trade liberalization, privatization and financial market deregulation). The 'pro-globalizers' believe free trade between nations, with no protective barriers, to be the most effective way of increasing global wealth and of lifting poorer countries out of poverty. It is incontestable that market capitalism has led to increasing global wealth, as the proportion of GDP traded internationally has risen from 5% in 1946 to 25% now. The Sachs/Warner study from Harvard University found that developing countries with open economies grew by 4.5% a year in the 1970s and 1980s, while those with closed economies grew by 0.7% a year.

Pro-globalizers regard those who argue against globalization as idealistic and naïve, and as failing to understand the complexities and ultimate benefits of the financial system. They believe that those who would stop markets acting efficiently (by making a special case for poor countries) will in the end destroy the wealth of those nations. Take, for example, flower-growers in Uganda, who produce flowers for export to Europe. It is hard work, but it pays better than subsistence farming. Not only do Europeans get flowers in winter but the Ugandans eat better and are able to school their children. In other words, it may be a tough option, but in the long run joining world markets is the only way to create wealth (The UK Department for International Development is an example of a body taking this view). Such people also argue that many countries are held back, not by unfair terms of trade, but by internal corruption or by the lack of an economic infrastructure that would allow them to deliver the goods in world markets.

'Anti-globalizers' see the gap between rich and poor widening and blame the growth of global capitalism for that gap. Today more than 800 million people do not have enough to eat and where the income gap between the top and bottom fifths of the world's people jumped from 30:1 in 1960 to 74:1 in 1997. They point to the ecological problems inherent in global trade and call for a return to more locally-based economies.

Our Ugandan flower-growers would question whether, overall, they are better off. Yes, they might have more money, but they now have to buy the basic goods they would have grown, which are now sold more expensively because demand is high. They are now at the mercy of market prices, and the chemicals they use to grow the flowers are threatening both their lands and their health. They might also ask why there was subsistence farming in the first place.

People on this side of the debate point out that the collapse of communism has led to a much more ruthless kind of capitalism. They see that the way to change the operation of multinationals is by exposing their practices in the press and by protesting publicly about their power. This side of the debate wants massive intervention to stop poverty caused by capitalism, and wants partnerships between nation states, charities (non-governmental organizations: NGOs), multinationals and global agencies to bring about reform (one of the key voices on this side is Joseph Stiglitz: see his *Globalization and Its Discontents*).

Pro-globalizers point to the massive benefits that globalization has brought us: freedom of movement, freedom of communication, freedom of consumer choice. Anti-globalizers talk about the 'McDonaldization' of the world; the rearing of the 'MTV generation' and the recognition of Nike and Disney as global symbols. Journalist Naomi Klein calls this the 'branding of culture': there is no space left any more that does not have a brand name attached to it. Every thing and every event comes at a price and with a logo (usually American). Pro-globalizers say this is rubbish; America does not hold the corporate power that is claimed. Furthermore, branding is not the manipulating evil that it is made out to be. Human beings have minds of their own and can choose what they do and do not buy.

The debate remains polarized and the arguments are often highly complex and technical. The reality, though, is that there is a middle ground that is trodden more often than is sometimes thought. Many anti-globalizers are not actually anti-globalization as such, but are against the current effects of economic globalization as presently managed by the International Monetary Fund, the World Bank and the WTO. Similarly, a commentator such as Philippe Legrain, coming from a staunchly free-trade position, would still advocate the need for debt cancellation, reform of the WTO, increased aid, capital controls, and for governments to do more to protect the vulnerable when people lose out from globalization.

One thing is clear: in our increasingly globalized world, the different issues involved in the problem must be seen as part of the wider whole, rather than as separate entities. As social scientist and theologian Peter Heslam says, 'The interests of the environment, economic growth, security and democracy are diverse but also interconnected and therefore need to be treated together, rather than in isolation.'

Technology has ensured that globalization is here to stay. Capitalism seems to be the best way forward for generating wealth, and no viable alternatives are being proposed. Rather than demanding the demise of globalization, the key is to channel it so that the rights of local people and their environment come before the rights of shareholders to increase their profits.

Globalization defines our world today and this whole book could be seen as looking at how to respond to it. But, does the Bible have any relevance here?

Biblically, there is nothing wrong, *per se*, with globalization. In fact, the Bible, too, has a global vision. Whether it is the foundational call of Abram (Genesis 12:3), the words of the prophets (e.g. Isaiah 49:6), the universality of Jesus' message (e.g. Matthew 8:11) or the inclusivity of Paul (Romans 14:11), we see a vision of the peoples of the world united in worshipping the God who made them.

Revelation brings the vision in all its glory to a climax. Before the throne of God stands 'a great multitude that no-one could count, from every nation, tribe, people and language' (7:9). At the heart of this scene is Jesus, the Lamb; the biblical vision finds its centre and fulfilment in him.

One of the implications of this universality of the Bible is that it goes right against globalization's treatment of culture. Globalization is often seen as destroying local cultures whilst promoting American culture. As the Bible unfolds, however, it is clear that every culture is acceptable and valid as a vehicle for God's revelation. This both relativizes and gives value to individual cultures in a way that globalization does not.

While globalization itself might be neutral, the biblical vision demonstrates that Christians have a global dream that is far more fulfilling than that offered by globalization. As Alex Araujo says, 'Globalization is the current strategy that a secular and lost humanity has developed to cope with an existence devoid of faith and hope in God'.

Author Tom Sine is particularly clear on the need to show people the Christian hope that can be brought to a world caught in the clutches of globalization and claims that 'the only way we can begin to contend with the seductions of McWorld is to offer a more compelling dream than the Western Dream'. This dream is of a new heaven and a new earth 'in which justice comes for the poor, the instruments of warfare are transformed into the instruments of peace and festive banqueting and celebration will welcome us home'.

Action point

- Look at the food you buy, the clothes you wear, the equipment you use. Where is it from? Develop an awareness of the interconnectedness of your life with other people and environments all over the world.

H IS FOR HIV

What was the biggest killer among women aged 25–39 years in New York in the 1980s? Amazingly, it wasn't cancer or homicide, but AIDS, which has become the most destructive disease humanity has ever seen. In 2007 there were about 33.2 million people living with AIDS; 2.5 million became newly infected that year and 2.1 million people died of AIDS. 68% live in sub-Saharan Africa, where it is now the leading cause of death (including for children under 5). Globally, 2.1 million children live with AIDS. It is thought that AIDS will eventually kill half of all 15-year-old Ethiopian, South African and Zimbabwean boys.

The majority of new infections are among heterosexual women aged between 15 and 24. In Africa, for every 10 men infected, there are 12 or 13 women. Incredibly, in one area in South Africa, 58% of women aged between 20 and 24 are HIV+. In Botswana and some other parts of southern Africa, more than 30% of pregnant women are infected.

The numbers are immense, but in each of those numbers is the individual suffering that must be borne by every person who contracts HIV and by every person who sees a loved one die from it. The psychological effects of the trauma cannot begin to be envisaged.

One of the key problems is the huge numbers of orphans that this disease is causing. Since the beginning, 13.2 million children have been orphaned. At the time of writing there are 15 million children under the age of 18 who have lost one or both of their parents. This places enormous strain on the wider family, particularly on the grandparents, who, in their old age, might find themselves having to support as many as thirty grandchildren. In Botswana, every income earner in the poorest quarter of households can expect to take on four more dependants.

Not surprisingly, therefore, HIV / AIDS has huge economic implications. The workforce of some African nations is being decimated as people cannot work, either through having the virus or through having to care for those who do. This is deeply affecting the annual per capita growth of Sub-Saharan Africa in particular. It is thought that 20% of GDP could be lost by 2020 in those countries most heavily affected.

What is clear in all of this is that AIDS is directly linked with poverty. AIDS not only leads *to* poverty, but is also caused *by* poverty.

Medicine is expensive, controlled by pharmaceutical firms from the wealthier countries. The struggle to pay for it is either impossible or strips families of money that should go on food and education. As one Zimbabwean doctor put it, 'Drug companies are only really interested in us as a potential market, and though our need is great, we don't count as consumers because we can't afford to pay their prices.' She went on to say, 'As a doctor it is hard for me to know that my patients may die of treatable diseases because our community cannot afford the medication. Imagine the pain a mother feels watching her child die of pneumonia, knowing that if she lived another life, if she had transport to the nearest clinic, if she could buy the drugs herself, the child might survive.'

Many healthcare systems in general are struggling. Once someone is infected with HIV, a lack of medicine increases the likelihood of other infections, including STDs. When the future looks hopeless, there seems little point in taking care with life; and young people do not take, or are unable to take, the necessary precautions.

UNAIDS (the Joint United Nations Programme on HIV/AIDS) describes AIDS as 'an index of existing social and economic injustices', and it is interesting how many of the factors involved in the globalizing of our world (see previous chapter) find expression in the AIDS crisis. Gillian Paterson, consultant on development and health issues, expresses it well: 'A society's vulnerability to HIV/AIDS is closely bound up with its lack of ability to resist global economic forces, including the results of structural adjustment, the debt burden, privatization of services, and WTO policies on intellectual property rights, trade and services.'

Because of this, UNAIDS' writings on what would be an effective response to help a nation reverse infection trends identify debt relief as being key. Alongside debt relief there needs to be recognition of how the policies of the WTO, the IMF and the World Bank impact on the poorest people and on HIV transmission rates. In order for this to happen there must be strong political support and leadership on these issues.

One of the main ways to tackle the situation is prevention through education, because, alongside poverty, promiscuity is a key factor in the spread of the virus. In particular, education should be targeted at young people, many of whom know little about AIDS. In some countries, UNICEF estimates that over 50% of young people aged 15 to 24 have never heard of AIDS or do not know enough to prevent infection.

Alongside young people, the education of women is also vital: another example of how women's rights play a central role in development. Adrienne Germain, president of the International Women's Health Coalition for the UN, says that 'men's demands for sex' are to blame, not any ignorance or promiscuity on the part of women: 'It is because men have sex with any number of women – and they bring it back to their wives'. Empowering women to be able to say no to sex, or at least to insist on the use of a condom, is essential.

Finally, responses to the crisis (whether prevention or care) are always most effective where they are local and community-based. In particular, these should involve those who are actually HIV+ themselves. In order for this and for any of the above to happen, we need to foster social openness and fight the stigmatism and prejudice that surround HIV/AIDS.

This brings us right back home, because we cannot see AIDS as something that is affecting only poorer countries. While the majority of cases are elsewhere (the UK infection figure is 0.11% and in the US only 0.6% of people aged between 15 and 49 are infected), we must not become complacent. This low percentage is largely due to the massive education programmes and initiatives that have worked so hard at breaking the stigmatism attached to the virus. But education needs to happen in each generation if it is to maintain its effectiveness.

The HIV issue touches on many biblical principles. We see it reflected in Jesus' refusal to bow down to the social conventions of his day, and in his compassion for those who were stigmatized and outcast (e.g. the man with leprosy, Mark 1:40–42). We see it reflected in the Old Testament's belief that the right of all to use the earth's resources comes before anyone's right to ownership (see 'C is for Creation'), and medicine must surely be a modern-day application of that. We see it reflected in the value that the Bible gives to women (particularly within marriage: 1 Corinthians 7:3–5) and to fidelity within marriage (Matthew 5:27–32). Perhaps most especially, we see the HIV crisis reflected in the biblical injunction to have a particular concern for the widow and the orphan (e.g. Deuteronomy 24:17–21; James 1:27). Whether through education, care or campaigning, there is much that we can do, nationally and internationally, to be responding to that call.

Action points

- Protest about WTO, IMF and World Bank policies that keep poverty as the driving force behind the spread of HIV. The organizations given in 'A is for Activists' will be helpful here.
- Pray for the advancement of research and for those people infected and affected.
- Promote and support the work of charities that work in this area (see website).

I IS FOR INVESTMENTS

CARE (Christian Action and Resource Enterprise) works to offer practical help and advice to those who are in need. They have a charity shop in the Cleethorpes and Grimsby area that provides jobs and training for those hoping to re-enter employment and receives donated household goods that can be sold or given to needy families. They also help in the areas of debt and welfare rights and provide a rent scheme that helps to house families.

In Chile, the cooperative Liberación is a savings and loan bank that promotes and strengthens small businesses and helps to create jobs. In Kenya, the Family Finance Building Society works with women and children in rural and slum areas, setting up micro-credit programmes to stimulate employment. Back in the UK, Organic South West is a regional advisory centre for farmers, growers and businesses, helping them with all aspects of the organic market.

All of these businesses have recently received loans to help them improve their work, from a bank attempting to operate on an ethical basis. Perhaps my money has played a part in the work they do?

By contrast, in another part of the world, a corporation's activities are destroying the livelihoods of the indigenous people in order to increase shareholder profits, while in a nearby UK village another local bank branch closes down. Perhaps my money has allowed this to happen?

Through this book we are looking at how we can use our lives to help the world. The good news is that what we do with our money can play a significant part in that. For those of us who are rich (on a global level), actively seeking to do good with our money isn't just a responsibility: it's a definite blessing!

In a later chapter we shall look at the wider subject of money. The principle guiding this chapter, though, is that the question of money is not just about how much we give, but also about what we do with what we keep. From this perspective, the topic of investments, for those of us who are in a position to have surplus money to invest, is an important one that cannot be ignored.

Most of us will have savings and investments in one form or another. That might mean just a current account, or we may have invested in the stock market. We may have ISAs, National Savings or bonds. The majority of us will, at some point, have a mortgage and a pension.

The first questions to ask are: Should a Christian have investments in the first place and, if so, what is an appropriate level? Does saving anything demonstrate a lack of faith in God's provision, or does *not* saving demonstrate a lack of prudence and good stewardship? The Bible seems to teach both (compare Proverbs 6:8; 21:20 with Matthew 6:19). Lest we answer too quickly that Jesus' teaching should always come before that of the Old Testament, we should not forget that he himself depended on the support of wealthy women and did not demand that Nicodemus or Joseph of Arimathea give away all their money in order to be his disciples.

The Bible gives two positive reasons for savings: first, we save in order to fulfil our family obligations (Mark 7:9–13; 1 Timothy 5:8) and, secondly, we save in order not to be dependent on anyone (2 Thessalonians 3:6–12). Alongside this is the continual and overarching reminder that we must use any money or possessions we have to help the poor (e.g. Ephesians 4:28). Nowhere does the Bible say we should invest simply to gain more money in order to become more financially secure (look at the Parable of the Rich Fool in Luke 12:13-2!).

This does, of course, still leave room for interpretation as to what it means. How far does our family extend? How much should we leave our children? How much do we need to live on in order to avoid dependence? In this, as with so much, the Bible's teaching gives us parameters, but not a single, universally applicable norm. The appropriate attitude to wealth would seem to depend on the Christian's situation and calling (for instance, to the mission field, to a dependent family, to singleness, etc).

What we need to remember at all times is our natural inclination to justify saving the most we can. We must always guard ourselves against the desire to accumulate as much as possible in order to make ourselves as secure as possible.

Beyond this, though, a further question to ask is *how* should we save: what forms should our investments take? Surprisingly, the Bible provides a fair amount of guidance on this matter. Looking after our money, as well as the rest of creation, is a key principle: taking personal responsibility ourselves, not just letting others control our finances for us, and also ensuring that any business activity we are involved with promotes the welfare of creation. Relationships are always central and placed above the accumulation of wealth. Accountability and openness are important, therefore, so that we know to what purposes our savings are being put. The Bible would seem to place a ban on interest. Finally, the Bible is clear that no money should be acquired at the expense of someone else or through dishonesty.

If these principles are followed, it will soon be apparent how starkly they stand in opposition to the accepted forms of investment that the majority of us as Christians follow today. For example, we too often hold shares in large companies where there is no local accountability or relational basis, and where interest is used as the means of making profit. Banks likewise give depositors no control over the use of their finances or over the way the bank conducts its relationships with its borrowers.

Perhaps most important for the purposes of this book is the fact that so much of conventional saving today is in companies that exploit their customers, their workers and the created world. As Christians, we have a responsibility to see where our money is going and to ensure that it is not being used to the detriment of others or the environment.

Our money might be invested in a wide variety of ways (some of which might not cause you a problem personally). However, it might be used for the production and sale of military hardware or nuclear power, or it might be donated to a political party or involved in pornography, the fur trade or tobacco production. It could be used by an oppressive regime that tramples on human rights, or it could be involved in intensive farming, environmentally destructive mining, the illegal felling of tropical hardwoods, or water pollution. Our money could be used for currency speculation, which can damage a nation's economy, or it might still be used to service a southern country's debt. We need to be aware of the power of our money and where possible be responsible to ensure it is being used in an ethical way.

Thankfully, we *can* do something and we *can* control what happens to our money, if we are prepared to expend some time and thought. 'Ethical' or 'socially responsible' investments are on the rise and increasingly easy to come by for all investment purposes, including mortgages and pensions.

The term 'ethical investments' covers a broad spectrum, and we should always investigate each investment option. Some options work 'negatively' (by not investing in particular concerns such as the arms trade or tobacco) whereas other options work 'positively' (investing only in companies that are specifically working for social or environmental enhancement). A third option is what's known as the 'best of sector' approach. This allows investment in *every* sector, but only on the basis of selecting the most ethical/environmental companies within them. So, for example, regarding oil companies, if BP is investing the most in renewable energy, then while it is a 'dirty' sector, it could be included. In general, one good point to look for is openness and transparency in how an investment option works. For example, Triodos Bank produces a regular newsletter for its investors that gives details of some of the different businesses and projects to which it is lending.

Some of us may own substantial sums of money. Remember, there are stockbrokers who have entire ethical/environmental research departments, who will sit down with a client and establish an individual ethical screen. Another option is to become a 'business angel'; people who invest money and become shareholders in small businesses, often giving advice and expertise too. This must be one of the best ways to invest any extra money we might have: there is a good balance of risk and return. Close relationships are often fostered, helping us know exactly where our money is going, thus enhancing our role as stewards.

However we choose to play it, the key is that, whenever we put some money into an account, invest in an ISA, apply for a mortgage or whatever, we have a direct opportunity to use our money to do some good in our world: and that can only be an exciting thing.

Action points

- Look at where your money is invested. Is it being used for good or harm?
- Take time to look into the different ethical options that are on offer (see www.lisforlifestyle.com for more details).
- Identify an area of your financial investment that can be improved ethically. Make the necessary changes to your arrangements and then inform your bank, mortgage lender or pension scheme manager of your reasons for the changes. When you have done this, identify a second area to change, and so on. Don't try to rush this process: give yourself time to make the changes gradually.

J IS FOR JOBS

Do you leap out of bed on a Monday morning, thrilled to be able to start another week's paid work, and do you come home on a Friday evening, despondent because the working week is over? Perhaps not!

Maybe though you are wondering what the subject of jobs has to do with this book. This is where we move into the area of simplicity, something we shall look at further in 'S is for Simplicity'. At its most basic, the idea of simplicity speaks for itself. It is about simplifying our lives in the face of our society's constant demands. It is about developing a life of awareness and rhythm that enables us to focus on our relationships with God, with one another and with the created world.

What simplicity teaches us is that being involved in God's heart for justice is not only about the specific things we do in that area, such as ethical investments and campaigning, but holistic, encompassing every area of our lives. For many of us, work (including travel) can take up 60% or 70% of our waking hours. It is what the biggest portion of our lives is given over to, and the thing that more than anything else can inform who we are.

The first thing we need to recognize is the difference between employment (including self-employment) and work (which can include voluntary work, that done by carers, and so on). Both contribute to the wider community; one is paid while the other is not. There are a number of different reasons for paid employment: earning money, gaining a sense of security, tradition, enjoyment, duty, serving others, learning, prestige and status, socializing, personal growth, success, creativity, fulfilment . . . Which of these apply to you? More broadly, work has two functions: the financial and the personal. For some of us, both of these functions may be met in our jobs. For others, our job may meet the financial need primarily, and the other types of reward are found in unpaid activities.

Considering our jobs in this way helps to free us from the fatalistic sense that we *have* to do whatever job we are currently doing, and opens us up to other possibilities. Why are we doing this job? Is this what we want to do? Is it what we believe God is calling us to do? Did we take this career path because of cultural expectations? Is our job a result of decisions made, years ago, that we were unaware we were making at the time?

Some of us have got ourselves caught up in the materialistic rat race. Ellen Goodman sums this up well: 'Normal is getting dressed in clothes that you buy for work, driving through traffic in a car that you are still paying for, in order to get to the job you need so you can pay for the clothes, car and the house that you leave empty all day in order to afford to live in it.'

Looking at our work in this way gives us the opportunity to reappraise the jobs we are in and ask ourselves if there are any changes that we want to begin to make.

John's story is a good example. He was a city lawyer, specializing in the investigation of international bank fraud, when he was first challenged about the claims of the Christian faith by a barrister. Three years of forensic investigation later, he accepted that what was written in the Gospels was true. But it made no difference because an intellectual faith is, in reality, no faith. He was in Hong Kong on a fraud investigation and heard the testimonies of some of the ex-heroin-addict former Triad gangsters who worked with Jackie Pullinger. Their tales brought it home: if Christ has risen, he is alive and at work today. This changed everything: John left law to work with Jackie Pullinger. Then he felt God calling him back to the UK. In time he set up a bank, working with people wanting to come off benefits and stand on their own two feet. From a large house in an upmarket part of London, he and his family moved to a bungalow in a run-down area. Their time was given to home-schooling their children and working with people in need.

John's story is not about moving from a non-Christian to a Christian option: investigating international bank fraud could be a high Christian calling. Rather, what John's story illustrates is his willingness to change when God asked him to.

While this kind of lifestyle change may be an option for some, for the majority of us our jobs simply help us keep our heads above water. Work in the UK is currently in crisis as people find themselves working longer and longer hours. In fact, Britons work the longest hours of any country in the EU. Research shows that many managers have no time for other interests and believe their work damages their health, and affects their relationships with their children and partner.

Our work-orientated society creates a world of skewed values in which human fulfilment is seen as being an escape from work. We work in order to increase our wealth, in order to achieve leisure. Work is thus rarely seen as an end in itself.

This is in direct contrast with the biblical testimony. Here, work (whether paid or unpaid) is good in and of itself: something that God ordained for people to do. In Genesis 1:26–28 and 9:7 we see that God made us to work. Work is an indispensable part of what it means to be human, and even God himself is described as doing work (Genesis 2:2 and elsewhere). Work is thus an important aspect of our self-fulfilment as people, rather than something to be avoided at all costs. The search for excellence and achievement is not disparaged, but positively encouraged (as seen, for example, in the building of the tabernacle in Exodus 35).

At the same time, however, work is not the means to salvation; and there is a negative side to it, as seen in the curse of the fall. Work can be hard and painful (and certainly it can be used for wrong ends) rather than positive creativity.

Work is not the be-all and end-all: God's week of creation finished with a day to rest. Our lives should have a rhythm to them that includes time set aside to rest and time that is specifically dedicated to worshipping God. Our calling (our 'vocation', if you like) is not limited to work; it also includes friendship, play, love, worship and rest.

Because of faulty theologies that have permeated the church (particularly those that created a sacred–secular divide), we see our workplaces as necessary for our survival, as opposed to our churches, which is where the *real* work of being a Christian takes place. Thus we may spend many hours of our day working in the supermarket, but it's the two hours that we spend running the youth work that get the attention. Instead of this, we need to develop what Mark

Greene describes as 'faith consciousness': a deliberate awareness of God's presence in our workplaces and an integration of our faith, our work and the rest of our lives.

The challenges that our workplaces offer us are many. We might find ourselves working in areas that perpetuate the problems that we are looking at in this book, and where the rightness of our remaining is questionable. One of the most challenging aspects of Christianity is that often there are no hard-and-fast rules, but guidelines to follow and the Holy Spirit to prompt. This applies here too. God will call some of us to work within the structures that perpetuate the injustices we have looked at so far in this book. Look at Daniel. Look at Joseph. This is no easy calling: it comes accompanied by its own pressures and frustrations, working out where compromise is the right route and where it is not. God will call others of us to find work that brings us outside the structures. Look at Amos. Both positions will give us opportunities to critique and to live and speak prophetically. But, wherever we stand, we must do so knowing that this is where God has placed us.

Action points

- Is there an attitude about your work that you need to change? Do you know that you are where God has placed you?
- Is there some way in which you might be able to help your place of work become more socially and environmentally friendly?

K IS FOR KIPPERS

Our local fish'n'chip shop informs its customers that all its cod comes from Icelandic waters and not from the North Sea. The owner told me that so many people had asked him about it, and he had seen his sales starting to fall, so he realized he had better do something about it.

The saga of the humble cod has become symbolic for what is happening in our seas. At the beginning of 2003 the 'State of the World's Fisheries and Aquaculture 2002' report (SOFIA) revealed that nearly half of the world's marine stocks have been fully exploited and there is no expectation that they will expand again. In particular, cod levels in the North Sea (from where our fish 'n' chip-loving nation has traditionally got its cod) are at their lowest level ever and seem in danger of complete collapse.

The modern practice of trawling (whereby weighted nets are dragged across the sea floor to catch prawns and bottom-dwelling fish) is one of the main reasons for the decline of fish stocks. Trawling destroys the thick natural carpet of plants and animals that live on the floor, necessary for the survival of the fry of fish such as cod. Trawling is indiscriminate in what it catches; it can damage or destroy species such as corals and sponges that take years to recolonize. Prawn (or shrimp, as they are called in the US) trawling is of particular concern, since it is responsible for one-third of the world's discarded catch, and up to 25% of seabed life can be removed by the pass of just one prawn trawl.

The global fishing industry is huge, worth $55.2 billion in 2000 and $71.5 billion in 2004. Its most significant feature is the rise in aquaculture, where fish and seafood are farmed rather than being caught wild. Aquaculture is the fastest-growing sector of all animal food production, growing from 3.9% of fish supplies in 1970 to 29% (48.2 million tonnes) in 2001 to 33% in 2005. On average, it has grown by 8.8% a year since 1970, compared with meat production, which has grown by only 2.8%.

Around a third of the fish and seafood we buy will have been raised in fish farms, and this proportion is growing as we demand increasing amounts of fish and seafood in the face of declining wild stocks. Since salmon and prawns are two farmed species that are particularly popular in the UK, it is helpful to look more closely at what is involved in their production.

As we saw in 'F is for Food', salmon has moved from being a luxury to one of the cheapest of meats. In Scotland, the retail value of the salmon industry is nearly £700 million a year. But this is coming at a price. One key concern is the amount of chemicals that are used in salmon-rearing. Around thirty different chemicals are licensed for use on fish farms, including an artificial pigment to make the naturally grey flesh pink. Since 1997, government scientists have detected chemicals including DDT in farmed salmon. Salmon-farming is polluting because old water containing high concentrations of chemicals and fish faeces is flushed out in exchange for new. In 2000/2001, 10,000 km^3 of Scotland's west coast were closed to scallop-fishing due to high levels of Amnesic Shellfish Poisoning. During the summer of 2000, 57 of the 60 areas closed were in salmon-farming areas. All of this makes the simple point that the only salmon we should be eating from Scotland is that which is certified organic and hence can be guaranteed to have been well managed.

So what about wild salmon? Sadly the situation here is not much better, though from a different perspective. Salmon stocks in many parts of the North Atlantic are in *serious* decline. Many measures have been put in place to reverse this trend and restore the stocks, such as restrictive management measures and reductions in fisheries and exploitation rates. So far, however, the salmon has not responded. The only wild salmon, therefore, that we should be eating is either Pacific salmon that carries the MSC logo or Atlantic salmon that has been sustainably harvested. At all costs we must avoid Atlantic salmon that is not able to make that guarantee.

Above, we saw the damaging effects of prawn-trawling. Unfortunately current farming practices are not much better. Some of the issues are similar to those regarding salmon: prawns are farmed intensively, using high levels of feed, pesticides, antibiotics and other chemicals in order to maximize profits and combat disease. The resultant pollution is horrendous. In Thailand, prawn ponds discharge around 1.3 billion m^3 of effluent into coastal waters each year. Of particular concern is the loss of coastal habitats and the damage done to nearby marine ecosystems such as coral reefs.

Mangrove swamps in Africa and South-east Asia have been cleared in a manner similar to the clear-cutting of the rainforests (see 'P is for Paper') in order to make room for prawn ponds. From 1987 to 1993 Thailand lost more than 17% of its mangrove forests to ponds. This degradation has left coastal areas exposed to erosion, flooding and storm damage (as witnessed in the awful effects of the tsunami which are thought to have been exacerbated because of the lack of mangrove forests), altered natural drainage patterns, increased salt intrusion and removed critical habitats for many aquatic and terrestrial species. Ironically, 2 kg of fishmeal (often sourced from low-value fish caught wild) is needed to produce 1 kg of farmed prawns.

However, there are now prawn farms, though few-and-far-between, that are being managed sustainably. The current advice is that we should return to thinking of prawns as a very occasional and expensive treat. If you do buy them, make sure they are organic or Madagascan tiger prawns (Madagascar is working towards making all its prawn fisheries sustainable, so is a better choice than other countries). The only country from which you can currently buy certified organic tiger prawns is Ecuador. They are stocked by Waitrose, which asserts that all its warm-water prawns are fully traceable back to their farm of production, and that the farms are all environmentally and socially sustainable. I leave it to you to find out which other supermarkets offer such prawns and to make sure these are the only prawns you buy!

The good news is that, in general, our supermarkets are taking notice of many of the issues raised in this chapter, and the majority of them now source their cod and haddock from sustainable fisheries (i.e. line-caught from Icelandic waters). In 2006 Wal Mart contributed significantly by committing to source all its fresh and frozen fish from MSC-certified sources by the following three to five years. Asda, Wal Mart's UK arm, has matched this commitment. Not surprisingly, this has had a noticeable 'ripple' effect on fisheries, processors and retailers. In the UK, M&S has committed to sourcing all its fish and seafood from MSC-certified sources or the equivalent by 2012, and Waitrose do not sell any products that are on the MCS's 'to avoid' list. British consumers have responded likewise, and the latest figures show that the market for sustainable fish has grown by a massive 224%! Other supermarkets still have a long way to go, however – particularly regarding salmon and prawns – and it is up to us as their customers to insist that they follow in the footsteps of these leaders.

In the creation story we are told that God caused the water to 'teem with living creatures' and blessed those creatures and commanded them to be 'fruitful and increase in number and fill the water in the seas' (Genesis 1:20–22). We can be extremely thankful that he did so, as there is no doubting the delight of eating those fruits of the sea, and their healthful benefits. Whether we enjoy them from the supermarket or at the restaurant, we must take responsibility to ensure that our pleasure is not working against that blessing and at the expense of God's world.

Action points

- Carry with you the MCS's *Pocket Good Fish Guide*: only buy fish/seafood that is in its 'Fish to eat' list and never buy any that is in its 'Fish to avoid' list.
- Ask your supermarket where the fish and seafood you buy comes from. Congratulate them where they are getting it right and ask them to change where they are not.

- Develop an awareness of how your activities might impact on the seas, however far away they seem. See 'F is for Food' and 'R is for Recycling' for more information on intensive farming, plastics and sanitary products.

L IS FOR LETTERS

'Oh, no! Not another one from that Mrs Valerio . . . !'

I sometimes wish I could be a fly on the wall in the customer services office at our local supermarket, because I can imagine that response as they go through the week's comments cards. I once read that we should become a nuisance to our supermarkets, asking questions about their policies and practices and badgering them about the issues we feel are important. After all, I reason, they take so much of my money every week, it would be rude not to give something back in return!

So I try to let them know my concerns at every possible opportunity. Mostly that is through the comments cards that are available at the customer services desk. I don't use them every week, but, if I read something I would like to ask them about, or see something that worries me, I take a few minutes to fill in a form. The nature of the reply depends on which particular supermarket you use: whether it is positive or negative, open or defensive. As suggested in 'F is for Food', it can be interesting to ask the same question to different supermarkets and compare the responses. More often than not, the reply will lead to my writing my own reply, and soon a regular exchange over a particular issue emerges. This often leads to the query being passed on to head office, where it is dealt with directly.

Mostly I feel like I'm banging my head against a brick wall – but not all the time. I have had some successes (see B is for Bananas). It might just have been coincidence, but I like to think that my letters and emails contributed to these policy changes.

It is easy to feel on my own, but actually this is far from the truth. When I was in the middle of my tennis game of emails with Tesco over fair-trade bananas, a friend mentioned that she was also writing to them about fair-trade bananas. That was encouraging! Actually, I didn't realise it but there were people all over the country putting pressure on Tesco.

'Letters' covers a number of different methods of communication: yes, letters, but also emails, phone calls, postcards and now even Facebook campaigns (see Tearfund's SuperBadger application). Postcards, in particular, have become increasingly popular, with all the main campaigning charities using them as their chief weapon. These organizations recognize that many people are too busy to write a proper letter. A postcard with the text already on it, which we can sign and send, is an ideal way to motivate people to do something and to get the message across that people care about the issue at hand.

Another good way of applying pressure is to write into the readers' section of the local paper. Martyn Williams, Parliamentary Co-ordinator for Friends of the Earth, told me,

'When I worked for an MP, scrutinising the local paper was crucial. If a campaign was doing well in the local paper, we knew we had to sit up and take notice.'

Encouragingly, these methods are proving to be remarkably effective.

One of the best examples of a successful online action is The Big Ask campaign for a climate change law. In November 2006 a climate change bill was announced in the Queen's Speech. This was the result of over 130,000 people sending messages (postcards/emails) to their MP and asking them to back the campaign by signing up to Early Day Motion (EDM) 178. A total of 412 MPs signed the EDM, which is equivalent to 64% of MPs overall and a majority of every party sitting in parliament.

Writing letters and sending emails and postcards really does make a difference. As the Catholic aid agency CAFOD says, 'Writing to politicians does have a big impact. It is the easiest way to gauge the level of public interest on one particular subject. The more postcards land on the desks of MPs and senior politicians, the more seriously they are going to take that subject.' In addition, sending a card with a charity's logo on it helps the lobbying work done by that particular organization as they then gain recognition and legitimacy through demonstrating public support.

Amnesty International told me of the effect letter-writing had for one man:

I was being kept naked in an underground cell. When the first 200 letters came, the guards gave me back my clothes. The next 200 letters came and the prison officers came to see me. When the next pile of letters arrived, the director got in touch with his superior. The letters kept coming, 3,000 of them, and the President called me to his office. He showed me an enormous box of letters he had received, and said: How is it that a trade union leader like you has so many friends all over the world?

Many of the big issues are, ultimately, determined by the decisions of the big companies and by governments. But they depend on us for their support. Big businesses are constantly pressurized by the need to be producing the next dollar for their shareholders, and they need to know that there are people who care more about other people and the environment than about making money. We demonstrate this by our actions, but that care also needs explaining in words. If I switch supermarkets, the financial loss of my weekly shop is insignificant. If I write and explain why I am taking my loyalty elsewhere, however, and if they hear of others doing the same, it is more likely that they will begin to take notice. It is good to remember also to write to companies that we think are good and encourage them along the road they are taking.

Letters *are* the most effective form of communication, because they are personal and because they take time and hence represent commitment to the issue. But they *do* take time! I never have that time available and so I have to make it. It is a good idea to set aside one evening every other month, or every three months, to be your 'letter-writing evening'. Over those months you can collect together campaign ideas and then, on that evening, sit down and work through them, doing all the letters at one hit. It is easy to let it slip, so make that evening sacred!

Getting involved in this kind of campaigning work is all part of being an advocate: speaking up on behalf of those who cannot speak for themselves (Proverbs 31:8–9). It is an integral part of 'spending ourselves on behalf of the hungry and satisfying the needs of the oppressed', and it works alongside the kind of lifestyle changes that we have been looking at so far. It is important and necessary work that is more than worth the time it takes to put our finger to the keyboard.

Action points

- Get your diary and schedule four letter-writing evenings for the next year.
- Look back over the issues is this book and choose two topics of particular concern to you. Contact the relevant organizations and begin to get involved in their campaigns. Many organizations allow you to subscribe to email newsletters. These can be a handy way of keeping in touch.

M IS FOR MONEY

I ran a seminar recently on 'Discipleship and money' at a gathering of Christians from all over the UK. I led the seminar with a fairly dour, be-suited businessman. My word! I have never heard someone speak so passionately on the subject of money – about the excitement of having a radical attitude of detachment from money and the effects it has on our lives. At one point he even broke down in tears! Has anything so exciting ever been talked about in your church?!

It is a happy coincidence that the two central letters of the alphabet give us, in this book, the two topics of money and consumerism ('N is for Needs'). Truly these two things are what make our world go round today. Money, in particular, is so often at the centre of our lives; it can form who we are, how others think of us and what we are able to do.

In this book we are considering how we can be Christian activists, spending ourselves on behalf of the hungry, and the part our lifestyles play in this. So many of the issues involved with this revolve around our understanding of money and possessions. This understanding can easily be moulded by the culture in which we live. But, as followers of Jesus, we want our understanding to be based on him and on the rest of God's revelation in the Bible.

In 'C is for Creation' we saw how God created the world – and created it *good*. It is a totally positive account: no repudiation of the material world, but a thorough embracing of it. The fall, however, placed curses on the blessings and fullness that were there for people to enjoy.

Throughout the Old Testament two strands appear regarding money and possessions. On the one hand, there is nothing intrinsically wrong with having either, and, indeed, some parts of the Old Testament see them as part of the promises of Yahweh for those who live according to his ways (e.g. Leviticus 26:3–5; Deuteronomy 28:1–14). God is seen as a God of tremendous blessing and generosity: a God who rescued his people *out* of poverty, rather than calling them *into* it! Wealth creation is a positive calling that God gives people, and to be denied that ability can be a denial of God's purposes for our lives (e.g. the story of Joseph in Genesis 39:2–6, and Proverbs 3:9–10). We have been placed in a world full of plenty, and our response should not be to reject that plenty, but rather to look after it effectively.

On the other hand, wealth is not necessarily seen as a reward for covenant faithfulness, and other voices in the Old Testament warn of its dangers (as is evident in the lives of many of the kings, who 'did evil in the eyes of the LORD'). Note, too, that material blessing as a necessary reward from Yahweh is one strand of teaching that we do not see in the New Testament. In particular, the Old Testament makes it clear that a person's money or property should never be gained at the expense of another, who is thereby left in a poorer state. The prophets provide us with a strong denunciation of the gross inequality that arose within Israel (e.g. Ezekiel 22:29; Amos 8:4–6).

When we turn to look at Jesus, we shall be disappointed if we hope to find him concerned only with individual piety. Giving is as important to him as praying and fasting (Matthew 6), and he talks more about money than about anything else apart from the kingdom of God. He was very clear that we cannot serve both God and mammon/money (Matthew 6:24) and taught strongly about the dangers of money. He described riches as a strangler and as a worry (Luke 8:14; 12:22–34). Money can blind us to the eternal realities of life, and can indeed be a curse for us (Luke 16:19–31; 6:20, 24).

More positively, we should not be preoccupied with money because we should *seek first* the kingdom of God (Matthew 6:33). In a wonderful passage, Jesus challenges head-on our society's obsession with material things (our 'treasures') and instead puts before us the values of the kingdom (Matthew 6:19–34).

Jesus' message of radical kingdom economics is summed up in two incidents in the gospels. First, Zacchaeus shows us a person who, before meeting Jesus, put all his trust and value in his wealth (Luke 19:1–9). Martin Luther once said, 'Every person needs two conversions: one of the heart and one of the wallet', and here we see these two conversions working together. Zacchaeus' money was earned at the expense of the poor people of Jericho and he knew that the only appropriate response on meeting Jesus was to give back all that money – four times over! We can only guess at the financial effects of giving away half his possessions to the poor and then paying people back four times: it is unlikely that he would have been rich after that. Here was no giving away of his surplus; this was a radical outworking of the Jubilee principle.

The second incident is Jesus' observation of the widow who gave away her two very small copper coins (Luke 21:1–4). In contrast to the wealthy people putting their gifts into the temple treasury, Jesus recognized that 'this poor widow has put in more than all the others'. Again, we see how different the values of the kingdom are from the values of society. In our world, it is size and numbers that count; we are praised for the amount we give. In Jesus' eyes, what matters is how much we have left afterwards and the sacrifice that we have been prepared to make.

The early church continued Jesus' economic ethic, as the pictures given in the early chapters of Acts bear out. What is envisaged here is not communal living with the abolition of private property – clearly, people throughout the early years of the church owned their own houses and fields – but a community that put others' needs before their own and where members were prepared to give of their own possessions and money in order to see others' needs met. The call was both to share God's blessings with his followers and not to neglect the poor with whom they came into contact.

Paul uses the collection for the church in Jerusalem as an opportunity to demonstrate that Christians' attitude towards money, and their use of it, is not a peripheral issue. In his letters we get a glimpse of the early church reaching more into the middle and upper classes.

In particular, the church at Corinth ran into problems when people expected to be able to use their wealth to buy power within the church. Paul again sets out the contrast between Jesus' way and the world's way. James picks this up and his words contain a strong challenge for us today. Do we treat people differently according to their financial status? How does our faith outwork itself? (James 2; 1 John 3:17.)

What does all this mean for us today? It means that we may well need to make some changes in our attitude towards money and possessions. We shall look at this more broadly in our next chapter, but it needs stating that the biblical position is so far removed from what our culture tells us that we need continually to check ourselves and see in which camp we stand. Of particular note here is how far we are willing even to talk about the subject. A Joseph Rowntree Foundation survey found that 95% of those surveyed thought it offensive to be questioned on how they spent their money and whether the choices they were making could be improved on. Would you have put yourself in that 95%?

Discussing my finances is certainly something I can get prickly about. Nevertheless, I have two good friends who know all about my financial situation. The three of us have sat down and gone through our budgets with one another: our monthly expenditures and incomes; our savings; our mortgages; our pensions – everything has been laid out on the table and opened to one another for questioning and as a family we are trying, slowly, to bring our financial practices and attitudes more into line with what we see in the Bible. We are far away from the ideal and shall be working on this for the rest of our lives, but the best way we can do it is with friends around us who will question and/or support any decisions we make.

Edgar Hoover said, 'A budget tells your money where to go, otherwise you wonder where it went.' On a practical level, one of the best things we can do is sort out our finances so that we know exactly how much money we have, what we spend, what we save and what we give away. When we do this, we can begin to see where there might be areas of weakness that we can work on, and where we might have money that we can use to help others.

This is exciting stuff! I know of one couple with a good income who live very simply. At the end of each financial year they look at what they have earned and what they have spent and give the surplus away. Last year they gave away £45,000. For others of us it might be a question of putting a small amount of money aside each month and then giving it away when it has reached a certain amount. Perhaps we might impose on ourselves a 'luxury tax' whereby whenever we buy something that is a luxury (a bar of chocolate, cinema ticket, even a car) we buy two and give one away, or give away the equivalent sum of money.

Whatever we do, our aim is to discipline our attitude towards money and our use of it to bring it into line with the Bible's teaching, so that we might use as much of our money as possible to be a blessing to others.

Action points

- If you do not already do so, work out a budget so that you know exactly what your money is doing (Credit Action can help on this – see www.lisforlifestyle.com).
- Get together with a mature Christian friend and show him/her your budget. Ask your friend to comment and advise.
- Take one step that will help you use your money more for the benefit of others. When you have done that, take another step!

N IS FOR NEEDS

A friend of mine came round to see me recently. As she walked in, I absentmindedly looked down at her shoes. Instant reaction: 'Oh, don't look!' she exclaimed. 'I bought them over the weekend and I have so many pairs already. I knew I shouldn't, but once I'd seen them I couldn't put them out of my mind till I'd got them.'

Finally she admitted, 'Ruth, I think I've got a problem. I can't stop buying things. Even when I know I shouldn't, I just give in. I've got no control over myself and I need to get it sorted.'

My friend's confessions are nothing astounding and would certainly be echoed by countless millions around the world – and probably by many of us reading this book. Gandhi once said, 'There is enough in the world for man's needs, but not for man's greed.' This encapsulates the subject of this chapter: consumerism. For consumerism has taught us to blur the edges between what is a need and what is, if we are honest, just a greed.

Consumerism has been specifically cultivated over recent decades. To put it at its simplest, it is the culture whereby our primary activity and focus is consuming things, rather than producing them.

In the post-war years there was an era of mass consumption as a productivity boom led to a capacity to supply goods and services that outstripped demand. The only way to deal with this was to stimulate that demand: in other words, to produce a desire to consume. This led to all the marketing ploys with which we are now so familiar: advertising, built-in obsolescence, the promotion of credit cards and the opening up of new markets such as the teenagers – and now the 'tweenagers' – and the high-earning young professional market. I gave a talk recently on consumerism and called out various advertising slogans, and wasn't surprised to find that everyone knew the products they referred to: the 'ad man' has done his job well!

This is not necessarily a negative thing. As we saw in 'G is for Globalization', we benefit from a wonderful freedom of consumer choice, and our consumption of goods can be a blessing that allows our needs to be met. Bishop James Jones makes the point that 'Christianity is a religion of consumption. We are natural and original consumers. The Garden of Eden is planted with food for us to eat. And when the founder of Christianity departed this life he gave his followers an act of consumption by which to remember him.' The danger, though, is that as we consume, so we ourselves are consumed by the ideology of consumerism that overtakes us.

The result is that consumerism is now the dominant force in our society and carries some very powerful values. A person's identity and significance are defined by what they consume, whether a house, a car, a holiday, a hair product, clothes or whatever. The advertisements all around us ensure that we know the difference between the driver of a Volvo or a Renault Clio, or between a Hamlet smoker and a Bacardi drinker. Thus goods are valued for what they mean as much as for their use.

In the past, the individual's identity was connected with their family, their faith, their values and their location. Now identity is primarily found in what we consume, and often a person will build their supporting community around their consumption habits. Think of your family and friends and ask yourself to what extent your bonding with them is deepened through the things you consume (dinner out, a shopping trip . . .). How much of your conversation is about activities or objects of consumption?

The consumer culture is profoundly individualistic and self-centred. In this way it is closely identified with post-modernity, which stresses the autonomy of the individual and individual's rights to have whatever they want and to be whatever they want. After all, the customer is always right.

Holding pride of place is money. Without it one cannot consume, and so money is endlessly presented as having the ability to bring status, power, freedom and hence that elusive prize: happiness. Indeed, happiness is what it's all about. Consumerism is, at its heart, the ultimate pursuit of happiness and fulfilment. It offers us a life in which nothing goes wrong. The road is always empty, the dish is always full, the colours are always bright, the clothes are always white, the hair is always perfect and the man nearly so.

We may laugh at this, but the reality is that consumerism has come at a price and has affected the most important areas of our lives. We approach our relationships through our consumer lenses. We try our relationships on for size to see if they meet our expectations and fulfil our needs. If they don't, we put them back on the shelf and try others. Our relationships suffer as we have to work increasingly longer hours to keep up with the pressure on us to consume more and more.

Religion, too, has succumbed to consumerism. People shop around to find the religion, or church, that fits them best. Commitment is at an all-time low: if it doesn't suit our needs we move on somewhere else. Consumerism affects our faith, and the danger for us is that we develop a compartmentalized Christianity that makes no connection between our faith on a Sunday morning and how we spend our money the rest of the week. Tom Wright warns of a Christianity that becomes 'focused on me and my survival, my sense of God, my spirituality, rather than outwards on God, and on God's world that still needs the kingdom-message so badly'.

The global picture of consumerism is of a world struggling to meet the demand for more, more, more. The fashion designer Katharine Hamnett teamed up with Cred a few years back to produce a teeshirt bearing the words, 'How you spend controls what happens on the planet.' There are many causes of poverty: sinful personal choices, disasters, lack of technology, Western colonialism, corruption etc, but we have to recognize that our consumerism is part of our world's unjust structures.

The positive side is that we do have a choice as to how we live our lives and how we spend our money. While we should cut down our consumption, we have already seen that when we do consume we have the power to do so in a way that actually helps alleviate poverty and reduce environmental destruction.

In 'M is for Money' we looked in depth at what the Bible teaches about money and possessions, all of which is of course relevant here too. What else does the Bible say that speaks into our culture? A key Old Testament law is the Sabbath. This laid down important principles regarding rest and trusting God. It speaks to our culture of incessant work, reminding us that our work is not the be-all and end-all and that *we* are not the be-all and end-all. It confirms that, rather than economic achievement, our relationship with God, with one another and with our world is at the heart of what it means to be human and, hence, is our ultimate destiny.

Matthew 6 is a passage that speaks directly to our situation. What do we put our security in? Is it in God's provision or our material possessions? Which is more important to us? What are we investing in for the long term? Do we have an eternal perspective when we consider these things? How important are clothes and food to us? Do we 'run after these things' rather than the kingdom of God?

An overriding biblical theme that is so important for us to recover today is that of contentment. Consumerism makes us think that we need more and more, creating a continual dissatisfaction that is temporarily expunged by a shopping trip. Its message is that we are not rich enough, beautiful enough or smart enough. In direct opposition, the voices of the Bible tell us to be content: 'Keep your lives free from the love of money and be content with what you have' (Hebrews 13:5; see also Philippians 4:11–12 and 1 Timothy 6:6–10). Contentment comes from being secure in the knowledge that money and possessions are not the focus of our lives: that honour belongs to Jesus alone.

In Philippians 4:11–12, Paul talks of being content whatever the circumstances: not just knowing when to say that we have enough, but being content even when things are hard. A positive understanding of suffering is needed, since we are bombarded with messages that tell us that it is our right to be healthy and wealthy and beautiful, and that personal fulfilment is based on these things. The reality of the Christian life is that Jesus promises no such thing. The Bible often represents the life of faith as a hard, unrewarding and even painful experience, and Jesus speaks of it as a cross. Rather than expecting to experience a carefree life with no suffering, Christians can expect instead to find the grace and strength to go through these difficulties knowing that, ultimately, they are victorious in Christ.

Romans 12:1–2 urges: 'Do not conform any longer to the pattern of this world, but be transformed by the renewing of your mind.' Nowhere is this more germane than in this chapter.

As followers of Jesus, we live by a story different from that told by our culture. We know that we do not need to be surrounded by 'stuff' in order to find fulfilment. As we simplify our lives and refuse to be shackled by the chains of consumerism, we shall discover a new sense of joy and liberation.

Action points

- Don't watch television for a week, month or year. Then ask yourself: Did I miss it? What happened instead?
- Sort through your clothing, kitchen cupboards or even your whole house (!) and box up anything that you don't need or use. If, after three months, you have not opened the box at all, give its contents away.
- When you go shopping, take this list of questions with you:
  1. Do I really need this product? Why?
  2. Is this an impulsive purchase or have I planned it?
  3. Have I done research to find the best product to meet my needs?
  4. Do I know the environmental consequences of this purchase?

5 Does this product meet fairtrade standards?
6 Can I borrow it? Share it with someone? Buy it second hand?
7 Was it made or grown locally, perhaps saving energy and packing?

O IS FOR ORGANIC

'Didn't we do this already in "F is for Food?"' In our chapter on food we did begin to look at the reasons for buying and eating more organic produce, but there is more to consider, and I want to look further at organic food in this chapter, as well as move it beyond this issue alone.

The one factor, in the UK at least, that always comes up alongside this subject is price, as organic produce is often more expensive than non-organic. Why is this the case? We need to ask ourselves, first, why non-organic food is so cheap. One reason is farming subsidies. These subsidies are calculated by the number of animals per hectare and the size of the cropped area: the higher the number, the more help the farmer receives. This inevitably favours intensive, non-organic farming.

The second reason is that the external costs that the intensive farmer creates is paid for by the taxpayer. These costs include those of cleaning up rivers contaminated by chemicals (which is then reflected in our water bills), repairing wildlife habitats, and coping with sickness and disasters caused by farming (such as BSE – which cost the British taxpayer £4 billion – and Foot and Mouth).

All these things are paid for by our taxes. It is estimated that an average family of four in the EU spends £16 a week on agricultural subsidies, on top of their food bills. Likewise, they spend an extra £11 a week on clean-up costs.

The third reason it is so cheap is that cheapness is what we expect and demand. In the first edition of this book I stated how, over the last thirty years, the percentage of our household budget spent on food had dropped, on average, from 24% to 16%. Now, writing this five years on, that percentage has dropped to just around 10%. We then choose to spend that money on other items and the average household now spends more money on leisure goods and services than on food and non-alcoholic drinks. Quantity, rather than quality, is thus what we have been given. While our supermarket bill may make the food look cheap, however, it begins to look less cheap when we consider the hidden costs that the taxpayer is having to cover. In this way we are paying for our food three times: once over the counter, the second time in subsidies and the third in clean-up costs.

Having considered the cost of cheap food, we then need to look at what goes into organic farming. To put it at its simplest, organic food is more expensive because it is more labour-intensive to farm without chemicals; the yields are often lower, and parts of the farm lie fallow each year to increase fertility and so cannot generate an income. The conversion process can be an expensive time; the farmer cannot charge the premium price for organic produce, yet the yields will be lower and the initial expenses higher. What results from this process, however, is farms that practise a high standard of animal welfare, with crop rotation, strong environmental practices and the use of skilled techniques rather than a dependency on chemicals.

The cost of buying organic can be a bitter pill to swallow for those of us wanting to support its development. When you consider the illusion involved in our so-called cheap food and then look at what goes into organic farming, however, there can be no doubt that organic food is worth the extra.

Many people now realize that being organic reaches beyond food alone. Around 250 million tonnes of 80,000 different chemicals are produced every year and are used in everything we meet: sofas, computers, TVs, detergents, paints, mattresses, toys, windows, tins, and so on. There is no doubt that the chemical industry contributes to our quality of life and we could not live the life we do without the use of many of these chemicals. The European Commission, however, states that only a proportion of chemicals used has been fully tested, and increasing evidence shows that some of them are damaging our health, leading to a whole host of problems, from earlier puberty to allergies. The recent drive towards organic is about reducing our exposure to these chemicals, and this reaches into every area of our lives. Here are three of the most important.

If organic food is a concern, the next logical step is to extend that into our *gardening* practices: there is little point supporting organic developments if you scatter slug pellets over your flowerbeds and douse your plants in insecticide! Gardening brings some of the most satisfying pleasures of life. What better way to garden than in a way that enhances the small ecosystem you have charge over; encouraging birds, bees and butterflies and providing space for local wildlife?

Another area is *cleaning products*. These are full of chemicals, some are very harmful both to the environment and to our health. Thankfully, there are now very good, environmentally friendly products, readily available in supermarkets and health food shops. When we know about the damaging effects of regular cleaners, how can we not use these products instead? As always, they can be slightly more expensive. If this is a particular concern, go back to basics and make your own cleaning solutions: bicarbonate of soda, for example, does a great job.

A third area is *beauty products*. It has been estimated that a woman can absorb up to 2 kg of chemicals a year through the products she uses on her skin. Generally we have no idea what has gone into them and there is little regulation. Sodium laureth sulphate, for example, is the second-biggest ingredient in most shampoos, shower gels and bubble baths, but is surrounded by controversy over possible negative effects. I am realising that, if I don't want to eat chemicals, then I don't want to put them on my skin either. As with cleaning, so also with beauty products: there are alternatives to buy and recipes to make, and great fun can be had finding out about them and experimenting.

Becoming more organic is part of developing a lifestyle that takes more care of ourselves and of the world that God has made. The Old Testament makes it clear that respect for the land that God has given us is an integral part of our relationship with God and with one another (see 'C is for Creation'). The encouraging news is that, as Michael Van Straten says, every step does make a difference:

Every family that encourages a household culture of organic living makes an even greater difference, by educating their children to live organically in the future. Every tiny saving of fuel and every purchase of organic food will help. Each of these small steps contributes to a reduction of toxic material in our environment and a lower rate of global warming.

Action points

- Find out more about the issues around organics by contacting the organizations involved in its promotion, such as the Soil Association and Garden Organic.
- Choose one food product, one cleaning product and one beauty product and change them to organic.

P IS FOR PAPER

As I sit at my table, I am surrounded by paper wherever I look. I use paper constantly through my day. The postman brings me letters; I write the milkman a note, scribble down a shopping list, print out a map for a speaking engagement . . . I am not alone in this. In fact, Britain is the fifth-highest paper-user in the world, despite its size, and Americans use more than 90 million short tons of paper and paperboard every year. That's an average of 700 pounds of paper products per person each year!

Our demand for paper is one of the key factors behind deforestation, which, in turn, is the second-highest contributor to climate change, only behind burning fossil fuels. Deforestation contributes to climate change through the carbon the trees absorb through photosynthesis: scientists describe rainforests as 'carbon sinks'. Thus they are one of the main ways in which carbon (in the form of carbon dioxide) is absorbed out of the atmosphere. Because they absorb so much, when forests are felled and burned, the carbon dioxide is released back into the atmosphere (as also are nitrous oxide and ozone). In this way, deforestation is responsible for 20–30% of all carbon dioxide in the atmosphere.

Tropical rainforests are not the only type of forest in the world: there are also temperate forests (in northern Russia, North America, Chile and Australia), boreal forests (in the cold north of Europe and North America) and temperate rainforests (on the west coast of North America). All of these contain huge varieties of wildlife and are increasingly under threat from our demand for timber and other resources. It is the tropical rainforests, however, that are particularly significant.

Tropical rainforests are the Earth's oldest living ecosystems: forests in South-east Asia have existed for 70–100 million years. While they cover a relatively small amount of land area, they house half of all the plant and animal species in the world. Scientists estimate that there could be as many as 30,000 plant species yet to be discovered!

They are incredibly rich in both medicinal substances and foodstuffs. A quarter of the medicines we use today come from rainforest plants and they have been indispensable in treating leukaemia, Hodgkin's disease, heart ailments, hypertension and arthritis, as well as being used in birth control. Even so, again, less than 1% of tropical plants have been examined thoroughly for their chemical compounds. It is thought that cures for cancer and AIDS may well be found in there.

Much of our food originated in the rainforests, including bananas, avocados, various nuts, chocolate, rice, tomatoes, cloves and corn (the full list is much longer). While all of these are now being produced away from the rainforests, the genetic material from the wild strains is needed to keep the modern stock strong and healthy.

While they may be far away, therefore, the rainforests are hugely important to us and are rich in resources. Yet they are facing intense pressure. All the primary (i.e. original) rainforests in India, Bangladesh, Sri Lanka and Haiti have been destroyed. Every second 2.4 acres are destroyed; 149 acres every minute; 214,000 acres each day (an area larger than New York City) and 78 million acres each year (an area larger than Poland).

Why is this happening? There are six main causes of deforestation, all of which relate to what we saw in 'E is for Energy' regarding human greed and selfishness. This demonstrates again how the environmental crisis is, fundamentally, a spiritual issue.

First, the most obvious cause is logging, due to the world's demand for wooden and paper goods. Take a moment to think through all the rooms in your house. How many of the contents are made from wood?

The second cause is farming: primarily to produce beef for richer countries, particularly in fast-food outlets and processed products. In 2007 America imported just over $1,000,000,000 of red meat products from Latin and Central America. Whether the forest is cleared for cattle-grazing or for crop-farming, the thin rainforest soil grows pasture for only a few years, and then cattle-ranchers and farmers are forced to move on, cutting down yet more forest.

Since writing the first edition of this book, two farming issues have become prominent in exacerbating deforestation: biofuels and palm oil. The production of both of these industrial monocultures has caused huge deforestation and environmental degradation, has involved the (sometimes violent) displacement of indigenous peoples and has seen land which would have been used to produce food for local people used instead to produce commodities exported to the wealthier countries. It will be no surprise to discover that the people who work on these farms are often subjected to poor conditions, chemical exposure and other abuses. As I write this, European bio-fuel production is beginning to slow down, but in the US it is still charging ahead. The palm oil plantations in Indonesia have caused such massive deforestation that, if left unchecked, the industry could cause the extinction of the orang-utan by 2017.

Thirdly, the rainforests are being increasingly mined for minerals such as aluminium and tin.

Fourthly, oil extraction threatens large areas. BP, Chevron, Shell, Exxon, Conoco Inc. and Occidental are all involved in 'exploring' different rainforest areas. The extraction leads to massive degradation and pollution, as well as affecting human rights as tribal territories are invaded.

Fifthly, in order for any of this work to happen, roads are needed for access and electricity for power, so hydroelectric dams are built that flood big areas of forest and displace the people that live there. It should be noted that all of this depends on the companies having enormous amounts of money, and the World Bank and some of our high street banks are involved in providing the necessary capital.

Finally, subsistence farming creates problems as poor farmers are forced to burn down areas of forest in order to grow crops to eat and sell. As with HIV / AIDS, so deforestation also is clearly linked with issues of poverty; with the uneven distribution of land and money. There is a direct link between deforestation and the global structures that we have noted earlier in this book. One example is Brazil, where international debt is repaid primarily through exporting cash crops. This leads to the inevitable clear-cutting of the forests to provide the land on which to grow the cash crops.

It won't be a surprise to hear that deforestation is causing enormous problems, not least to the indigenous people themselves who have lived in the forests for thousands of years. Many tribes have lost their homelands and been intimidated and murdered as they have tried to resist this happening. In Brazil, in 1500, 6–9 million people lived in the rainforests. Now there are fewer than 200,000. Poverty and disenfranchisement all too often result. As tribes disappear, do we lose something of the colour and variety that form the 'great multitude' worshipping before God's throne (Revelation 7:9)? Interestingly, an acre of rainforest land is thought to be over six times more financially lucrative if sustainably harvested for fruits, latex and timber than if clear-cut for commercial timber.

The environmental damage caused by deforestation extends beyond climate change. In 'E is for Energy' we saw the spiritual nature of species extinction, and deforestation is causing the loss of biodiversity that is resulting in an alarming rate of species extinction. It is thought that 10% of the world's species could disappear within twenty-five years because of the breakdown of rainforest ecosystems. Remembering what we saw earlier about medicine and food, this has implications for us too.

Is there anything we can do? As so often, the stakes are high and the other players powerful. There is much money to be made out of the rainforests, and vested interests do not give up those interests easily. Nevertheless, there are still actions that we can, and must, take if we are to stop these hugely precious areas of forest being destroyed.

While there are a number of different steps we could focus on (such as reducing our beef consumption, particularly from fast-food outlets and in processed foods), the most important priority is to cut down our use of paper and wood. Particularly with regard to paper, this is something that I have been working on, and now use almost no new paper at all. I re-use everything before it finally goes in the recycling box, including envelopes. I keep letters I have been sent if the paper is in good condition and I don't mind others seeing them, and then use the other side for my own letters. I finish the letters by saying, 'Please forgive the informality of re-using paper for this letter' and, so far, I've had no complaints!

Then, we must ensure that, when we do buy new paper or wood products, they come from 'sound' sources. Any wood you buy *must* have the FSC (Forest Stewardship Council) certificate on it. Be wary of labels saying that the wood comes from a 'sustainable source', and take the time and trouble to find out what this really means. It may be the case, but often old-growth forests (for instance, in Canada or Sweden) have been cut down in order to provide the ground. The new forests are often really just tree factories that cannot support the wildlife that existed in the original forests. By buying from these sources we are encouraging this to happen more.

Any paper you buy (including toilet paper and kitchen paper) should have the highest percentage of recycled content possible: post-consumer recycled content is best. You can buy paper products, as well as wood, that are certified by the FSC. By cutting down our usage, rather than cutting down trees, we shall know that we are doing our bit to help save these amazing parts of our world.

Action points

- Look at your use of paper. What steps can you take to reduce the amount you use?
- Vast amounts of paper are wasted through junk mail. The Mailing Preference Service will take your name off all mailing lists (except those of companies with which

you already have a relationship). Write to them at FREEPOST 22, London W1E 7EZ, or register on the website: www.tpsonline.org.uk.

- Don't buy fast food unless you can guarantee the meat wasn't raised in the rainforests. If you have children who are magnetically drawn to the outlets, take time to explain why you would rather not eat there.

Q IS FOR QUESTIONS

Charles Steinmetz, American mathematician and electrical engineer, said, 'No man really becomes a fool until he stops asking questions.' In many ways this entire book is based upon asking questions: why is organic food more expensive? Why is HIV / AIDS affecting millions of people, but not many from my country? Why does it matter what I do with my money? Do I have to fly there? Who is the loser here? Where have the sparrows gone? Why do more people binge drink? Is there another way of looking at this? Who made my jeans? How should I live? What does God require of me?

I hope this book will encourage all of us to keep asking questions because questions are what keep us moving forward; they keep changing us; they push boundaries and revolutionise situations. To be someone who asks questions is to be someone who is not content with the status quo. American economist Paul Samuelson said that 'good questions outrank easy answers' and we must be prepared to fight against those who will try to satisfy us with easy answers, and keep asking questions, questions, questions . . .

In this chapter I want to look at a question that I am *always* asked when I am speaking on the sorts of issues that we've been looking at in this book: a question that has been hinted at elsewhere, but would benefit from being considered further. And, as we will see, this good question indeed has no easy answers.

It is what I call the 'green beans from Kenya' question: ie, should we buy green beans from Kenya (say) in order to help poor farmers, or should we *not* buy them, in order to reduce our food miles and help the environment? Let us look at the different sides of the debate.

On the one side are those who say that we should always shop as locally as possible, encouraging trade to operate primarily on a localised basis, rather than internationally. This is not to say that we should never buy from overseas as, clearly, there are some goods that we simply can't grow here (coffee, bananas, oranges etc), but is more to say that when local is available, that is what we should go for. This has a number of advantages. Firstly, of course, is the benefit environmentally as food does not have to travel huge distances to reach our plates, hence reducing our 'food miles' and subsequently our contribution to climate change. Since about 20% of UK and European climate change emissions are related to food this can only be a good thing. On a more subtle level, localised food production can strengthen the links with our food and so help increase our awareness of ecological issues, hence making us more likely to act in positive ways towards the environment.

Beyond this, Duncan Clark, author of *The Rough Guide to Ethical Living*, makes the point that concentrating on the local helps with issues of food security and our long-term ability to feed ourselves. Again, this is positive environmentally as food transportation relies heavily on oil supplies, which may be dwindling. It would also have positive governance results as an emphasis on localised food production would encourage more local ownership and decision-making, hence fostering greater local responsibility.

From the perspective of the poor farmers in Kenya, it is argued that they are better off growing their own food for their own people, not relying on the vagaries of the global market. As with local communities in the economically developed countries, so too a greater emphasis on local food production would encourage people in Kenya to have more responsibility for their communities, rather than being at the mercy of World Bank and IMF policies. People everywhere, including those from poorer countries, should be encouraged to engage in making a living from things that they, or people in their geographical area, *need*, not what people in the rich world *want*. There is a recognition here that we have made communities in poorer countries dependent on us and therefore have to take most of the responsibility for working to see these countries implement transition schemes so they can change to working to fulfil their own basic needs. This needs to go hand in hand with diplomatic and other efforts to maintain and increase the co-operation and understanding between countries, ethnic groups etc.

However, on the other side are those who say that stopping buying beans from Kenya would deprive the Kenyan farmers of a livelihood that they desperately need. Currently, there are an estimated 1.5 million people in Africa who make their living from agricultural and horticultural exports to the UK. According to the Institute of Development Studies, household surveys in Kenya have shown that working in the horticultural sector has made people better off than if they were in subsistence farming. To put it bluntly, while we may dream of localised economies, the consequences of our unequal world mean that less developed countries simply *have* to export to the richer countries in order to make money to survive and develop.

What's more, the statistics on food miles are not always as straightforward as they may seem and it is generally the case that a food product grown in a low-income country will use less energy than that same product grown *out of season* in a high-income country. For example, fairtrade roses grown in Kenya *and flown to the UK* use almost 6 times less CO_2 than roses grown in greenhouses in Holland, demonstrating that food miles are as concerned with the methods of production as with the mode and distance of transportation.

People on this side of the debate also point out that food miles associated with the export of fresh fruit and vegetables from sub-Saharan Africa equate to only 0.1% of the UK's entire carbon emissions and that, if we are concerned with reducing our emissions, there are other more significant steps we could take instead. For example, Duncan Green, Head of Research for Oxfam, calculates that if everyone in the UK switched one 100W light bulb for a low-energy one, UK emissions could be cut by almost five times as much as would be saved by not purchasing fresh fruit and vegetables from Africa.

It is obvious, therefore, that this issue is far from clear and the debates around it will continue for a long while yet. What makes it harder still is that statistics on methods of production, mode of transportation and overall CO_2 emissions from any given product are not easy to come by, nor are the facts as to how many pence per product the producer receives, and these details are certainly not printed on the product in the supermarket, when you are holding it in your hand trying to decide whether or not to buy it . . . !

For me, this is part of the reality of living in a fallen world: a 'world of wounds', in which often the choices we have to make are not perfect. So, if you started this chapter with the anticipation of me concluding by telling you exactly what you should do, I'm afraid you are going to be disappointed! This whole area is extremely complex and also one in which our choices will be determined by our own individual priorities. So, if it were shown that the summer beans sold at my local farmers' market had produced fewer CO_2 emissions than those grown in Kenya, then there might be a simple choice to be made between environmental and developmental concerns. However, the point could also be made that, in the long term, climate change will wipe out any development gained by exporting to wealthier countries. The debates will continue . . .

Action Point

- Don't stop asking questions, especially the question, 'Do I really need this?'

R IS FOR RECYCLING

I went on holiday once to Indonesia, to see my brother, who was living there. We had a wonderful time travelling across the Indonesian islands. One of my most vivid memories was crossing from one island to another on a large local boat. There were quite a few bins, which people diligently used. As we drew near to the shore, I leaned over the side of the boat to take in the view: stunning white beach, clear blue coralled sea, coconut palms lining the beach – and watched as, to my horror, the crew took all the bins and one by one tipped their contents into the sea!

Waste is a problem that is facing all of us, wherever we live in the world. Those of us living in the richer nations might like to think that we are too sophisticated to tip our rubbish into the sea so blatantly, but the fact remains that, in the UK, we produce about 335 million tonnes of waste every year. 29 million tonnes comes from municipal waste, and the average person throws away their body weight in waste every three months! In the US, residents, businesses and institutions produce more than 251 million tonnes of waste every year.

Like the Indonesian boatmen, we can easily feel that this rubbish has disappeared and we need no longer think about it. But this couldn't be further from the truth: there is no such thing as throwing our rubbish *away*.

Just under 90% of UK rubbish is buried in landfill tips (compared to 55% of US rubbish). As the rubbish biodegrades, it produces carbon dioxide and methane (a greenhouse gas 200 times as powerful as carbon dioxide), contributing to climate change. It also produces a toxic 'leachate' that seeps into groundwater. In 1998, research showed that babies born within 3 km of toxic landfill sites, and potentially all landfills, were more likely to suffer birth defects than babies born elsewhere. In addition, landfill sites can give rise to problems such as increased traffic, noise, odours, smoke, dust, litter and pests.

Throwing so much away puts untold pressure on the earth's resources. Everything we use has to have come from somewhere and has to have been made from something, whether oil for plastics; sand, soda ash and limestone for glass; raw materials and minerals for steel and aluminium; or wood for paper and cardboard. As we have seen elsewhere, many of these materials are obtained in ways that damage the rest of creation, and often harm the people who live nearby.

The harsh reality in the UK, also, is that we are running out of landfill sites. In the search for alternatives, the authorities often turn to incineration as a solution. Those bodies promoting incinerators point to the fact that the energy they produce can be harnessed positively. The energy produced, however, is far less than the energy that is saved by recycling. Incineration, therefore, destroys valuable resources and leads to the use of more fossil-fuel energy in order to replace the products. It also undermines councils' recycling schemes, which demand a constant supply of waste in order to be economic. Some councils have even had to bring in waste from other areas and abandon their plans for waste reduction and recycling.

Incineration is also polluting. It produces emissions of particulates, heavy metals and dioxins, which are potentially dangerous to our health, and produces toxic ash, which then still has to be landfilled. Incineration does not even afford an employment opportunity, as it offers very few jobs compared with those offered by recycling. Overall, incineration is more costly than recycling and, as with landfill sites, noise and traffic become a problem.

No; the best solution is found in the three R's that have become the mantra of the environmental world: Reduce, Reuse, Recycle.

Reduce

E. F. Schumacher said, 'We tolerate a high rate of waste and then try to cope with the problem of recycling. Would it not be more intelligent first of all to try and reduce the rate of waste? The recycling problem may then itself become much more manageable.' We should try, at every possible opportunity, to reduce the amount we use, and hence the amount we throw away. As a general rule, anything with the label 'disposable' should be avoided, and we should always ensure that we buy things to last.

A lot of our rubbish comes in the form of packaging. Germany has seen a 12% decrease in packaging over the last five years, whereas the packaging industry in the UK is planning for continual growth. Buying locally produced food from local outlets is often one of the best ways of reducing the packaging we buy, as supermarkets so often go overboard in this area – particularly with processed food. If you've got the nerve, take off all the unnecessary packaging on products that you are buying and leave it at the checkout – or, preferably, with the shop manager! What we looked at in 'N is for Need' is relevant, since, if we always insist on the latest clothes and equipment, we shall inevitably produce more waste as we throw the old things out.

One little-discussed aspect is sanitary protection and the plastic and cardboard packaging that goes with it (not to mention the potentially damaging non-organic cotton used for its production). In the UK, over 3 billion sanitary towels, tampons and panty liners are bought every year, most of which are flushed down the toilet. As much as 50% of beach pollution consists of used sanitary protection. Sanitary protection should be put in the bin. In addition, there is a good range of protection that uses the minimum of packaging and is made from organic cotton.[(1)]

As you open your eyes to the issue of packaging, you may begin to notice practices of governments, councils and businesses – both locally and nationally – that go against the principle of reducing waste. Your local council recycling officer, your MP or government minister, and shop managers, are good people to whom to voice your concerns.

Re-use

In our disposable culture it seems so much more natural to throw something away rather than consider how we might re-use it and thus avoid wasting resources and energy on a new product. Plastic bags are a classic example – the scourge of our society! Have a policy never to accept one, and get into the habit of always having a couple (both carrier bags and fresh-produce bags) in your bag just in case you need one unexpectedly. The supermarket plastic boxes are excellent to use. Although the initial manufacturing is harmful, they are very long-lasting and useful for all sorts of things. I use them to put my recycling in and empty them at the recycling facilities at the supermarket before shopping. It has been great to see this issue gaining so much publicity in the years since I wrote this book, with many people now using cotton instead of plastic bags. The Republic of Ireland has led the way, taxing plastic bags and cutting their use by 90%. Let's hope that, when I write a third edition of this book, this will also have taken place in the UK . . . !

The near-universal use of 'one-stop' containers is another example of re-use. Containers for food, drinks, beauty products and cleaning products could all be designed to be refillable, thus cutting down on the vast quantity of cans and plastic that we dispose of each time we buy more of the same item. My local wholefood store is just beginning to introduce a refillable scheme for Ecover cleaning products. In Denmark, all drinks must be sold in returnable, glass containers.

If we have young children, an area where we can make a vast difference is by choosing re-usable nappies. Currently, disposable nappies account for 4% of landfill and this is becoming one of the major waste issues. Each nappy uses a lot of energy and resources in production and can take up to 500 years to decompose. Washing nappies is not the hassle that parents using 'disposables' tend to think it is. I know of friends using 'disposables' who do much more washing than I ever did! As *Go M.A.D!* says, 'Babies survived right up until the 1970s with cotton nappies. Why can't we all still use them now? They produce 60 times less solid waste than disposables. It's time to clean up our act.'

Recycle

Finally, when we have reduced and re-used as much as possible, we can see if we can recycle (and remember to buy recycled) too. Recycling is far more efficient in terms of energy and resources than landfilling or incinerating, and reduces the habitat damage caused by the extraction of raw materials. It promotes personal responsibility for the waste that we produce. It is good at job creation: for every million tonnes of waste processed, landfill creates 40–60 jobs, incineration 100–290 jobs, and recycling 400–590 jobs.

Almost everything we use can be recycled: our kitchen and garden waste, paper, glass, plastic, cans, foil, textiles, furniture, other household goods, batteries, wood, oil and tyres. Many of these we can dispose of easily through composting, recycling bins and kerb-side collection schemes. (If your council doesn't do one, make it a priority to press for one.) Other items may take more time and investigation (www.wastepoint.co.uk or www.recycle-more.com are good sites to visit). There may yet be some recyclable waste for which there are no local facilities. If this is the case, then ask your council to provide them.

The UK recycling record is dismal, but improving. Just under 90% of waste could be recycled, but currently only 11% actually is, far worse than in the US where 32.5% of waste is recycled or composted (an increase from 16.2% in 1990). One good news story is the increase in UK household waste recycling rate, which now stands at 32% and is improving all the time. The bad news story is in the non-household waste, which is what is dragging down the national recycling rate and is badly in need of reform.

All of this is our responsibility and part of how we take care of God's creation. After all, there is no such thing as waste in nature – the output from one organism is the input for another. As part of nature we too can take steps to make waste an irrelevant concept.

Action points

- Look at what goes into your bin. What is its highest content? Take steps to reduce that.
- Next time you go round the supermarket, make a note of all the excess packaging and unnecessary plastic and cans you see. Write a letter when you get home, or drop a note into the customer comments box, listing it all and asking them to reduce it and change their use of plastic and cans.
- Find out about the recycling facilities in your area. Are there gaps? If so, ask your council to fill them.

Endnotes

1 Natracare: 0117 946 6649. For more information on all of this, including re-usable sanitary protection, contact the Women's Environmental Network: 0171 247 3327.

S IS FOR SIMPLICITY

Do your toes curl when you hear the word 'simplicity'? Do you think of woolly jumpers and mung-bean stew? I can't say I blame you if you do, but I hope to show you that simplicity is actually about something far more exciting.

Henry Thoreau, one of the great writers on this issue, said that 'a person is rich in proportion to the things they can leave alone' and, in many ways, this sums up what simple living is all about. Partly, it's about our choices. As we look at our lives, do we know how we've ended up living how we're living, and why? What choices have we made that control our present lifestyle? When we wanted that new house or car, were we aware that the trade-off would mean working longer hours to pay for them and seeing less of the people we love? Too often we find ourselves on the treadmill of life, paying the consequences for choices we hardly knew we were making at the time.

Simple living is about stopping that treadmill and giving us the space to choose how we want to live our lives. There are many voices around us that tell us that happiness is to be found in good clothes and nice jewellery; in a job that commands respect; in crashing out in front of the TV in order to recover; in having a busy diary. Simplicity asks us to sit and listen to those other whispers inside us that we seldom have the time to hear. It helps us to discover the happiness that comes, not from having an abundance of money and things, but from having space for intimacy in our friendships, space for ourselves, space to live in a way that respects God's earth and, primarily, space for God.

Too often our days are spent thinking about the future: we drive the kids to school or drive to work while planning what we shall do that day, on autopilot, hardly noticing anything or anybody we drive past. As we talk to a friend on the phone, we are thinking about what we shall have for lunch and fail to hear what she is really saying. We shove a plastic container in the microwave and eat its contents while thinking about a later meeting, and miss the pleasure of eating good, simple food.

Simple living is about being joyfully *aware* of what we do and why we do it. We can live in the present as well as the future, having the room to savour each moment of our lives. Above all, simple living is about getting rid of the clutter in our lives so that we can hear the voice of God more clearly and serve him more readily. As we do that, we shall discover what it really means to be rich; for simplicity is not about meanness and poverty, but about true abundance (John 10:10).

Already, from what has been said so far, it will be apparent how this subject is relevant to the theme of this book. We might say that the concept of simplicity consolidates much of what we have looked at previously. Many people are recognizing that there is something wrong with our lives. We live in an extraordinary time, with communication and technical advances developing rapidly, medical science achieving 'miracles' and consumer choice at its highest, and yet with global inequality at an extreme. In the light of this, we have to ask ourselves the question that Micah asked (Micah 6:8): 'What does the Lord require of me?' In our world today, what does it mean to 'act justly and to love mercy'? How do I 'walk humbly' with my God? A Christian approach to simplicity provides a helpful answer.

As we saw in 'N is for Needs', our culture today is consumer-based. It is profoundly self-centred and individualistic, placing value in the things we possess and giving prestige to those who indulge themselves in luxury and waste. We have created a short-term, throwaway culture.

It is into this context that simplicity speaks. One of the key areas is our *time*. Time is God's creation and his gift to us. He has given it to us to enjoy and use for his service. We each have it in equal amounts, and how we choose to steward that time is our responsibility. Simple living allows time to be the most rewarding and beautiful possession that we have, helping us reach a place of wholeness and awareness both of ourselves and of God.

And yet, 'I haven't got time' is a frequently-heard complaint. As a result, many of us are suffering, with stress, sleep problems and relationship pressures becoming increasingly common. What is also clear is that the situation is only going to get worse. As writer, thinker and life-lover Tom Sine says, 'That means we shall have less time for family and friends, less time to pray and study Scripture and less time to volunteer to address the mounting needs of the poor in our societies.'

One of the greatest ironies of time is that time often seems to be directly disproportional to the amount of money we have. Time is one of the greatest dividers: between those who spend time to save money and those who spend money to save time. As Roy McCloughry has said, 'The new materialism is to do with our attitude to time.' Time has now become a status symbol; we measure our worth by our busyness and believe ourselves to be indispensable to all that goes on around us.

Our use of time reflects the values of our lives, and 'now' is a good time to ask ourselves whether or not we are truly living out God's values. If not, what needs to change? Many of us need to make changes so that we have the time simply to be: to be with ourselves and to be with God. Time in this sense has been described by Michel Schut as 'opening space in our lives for a greater awareness of God'.

For many, a helpful way for this to happen is through the practices of silence, solitude and contemplation. Let us touch the surface by looking at Gerald May's three suggestions as to how we can begin to create space.

First, he suggests looking for spaces that occur normally in our lives. Perhaps there are times that we automatically fill by turning on the TV or making ourselves a drink, but that we could make 'intentional': moments to stop and be still.

Secondly, we should try to find the more regular, set-aside spaces during the day that are 'simply and solely dedicated to just being'. However long, they are an opportunity to take some space and establish ourselves with Jesus at the centre.

Finally, May recommends building longer spaces into our lives for authentic retreat. These may involve actually going away for a retreat or just taking a day of quiet.

Our aim is to bring our use of time under control so that it serves our kingdom values rather than those of the world; living intentionally in each moment of time. Henri Nouwen's description of this is beautiful. He talks of a life

. . . in which time slowly loses its opaqueness and becomes transparent. This is often a very difficult and slow process, but full of re-creating power. To start seeing that the many events of our day, week or year are not in the way of our search for a full life, but the way to it, is a real experience of conversion. If we discover that writing letters . . . visiting people and cooking food are not a series of random events which prevent us from realizing our deepest self, but contain in themselves the transforming power we are looking for, then we are beginning to move from time lived as chronos to time lived as kairos.

Time is a good place to start a consideration of simplicity because it teaches us the importance of an inner simplicity, something we touched on in 'A is for Activists' where we saw the importance of prayer in our activity. As simplicity touches our approach towards money, the food we eat, the clothes we wear and so on, we remember that it begins with our heart attitude and only then moves on to our outward practice.

This book is about inspiring you to 'act justly and to love mercy'. Simplicity has these things at its heart and is desperately needed today. As Richard Foster says, 'Our task is urgent and relevant. Our century thirsts for the authenticity of simplicity; the spirit of prayer, and the life of obedience. May we be the embodiment of that kind of authentic living.'

Action points

- Foster has ten principles of simplicity:
    1. Buy things for their usefulness rather than their status.
    2. Reject anything that is producing an addiction in you. Learn to distinguish between a real psychological need, like cheerful surroundings, and an addiction.
    3. Develop the habit of giving things away.

4. Refuse to be propagandized by the custodians of modern gadgetry.
5. Learn to enjoy things without owning them.
6. Develop a deeper appreciation for creation.
7. Look with a healthy scepticism at all `buy-now, pay-later' schemes.
8. Obey Jesus' instructions about plain, honest speech. 'Simply let your "Yes" be "Yes", and your "No", "No"; anything beyond this comes from the evil one' (Matthew 5:37).
9. Reject anything that breeds the oppression of others.
10. Shun anything that distracts you from seeking first the kingdom of God.

Which of these strike you as interesting or particularly challenge you?

- How can you develop an inner simplicity?

T IS FOR TOURISM

I remember attending a tourist promotion with my husband, the sort where you are promised a free holiday if you sit through a presentation. Our poor sales rep knew he was on to a loser when he asked where we had most recently travelled to and we replied, 'Ethiopia'.

Somehow that wasn't a prime tourist destination. A few more questions later and it became clear that we weren't his average holidaymakers. Somewhat impolitely, he told us we were wasting his time and might as well leave right away. We were more than happy to do so and skip the two-hour presentation – and we still got a free break in Cornwall!

Our man got no commission off us that day, but I don't think he minded really. The room was full of people signing up to the promise of wonderful holidays abroad at a price they could afford. Everyone loves going on holiday: a time to get away from it all, relax, experience something different, perhaps enjoy some rare luxury. For many of us, our holidays are essential if we are to survive the busyness of our lives. As seen in 'G is for Globalization', one of the results of globalization is increased mobility, and we travel all over the world as tourists. As I write this, I have one friend travelling through East Asia and another holidaying in India.

Tourism is the biggest industry in the world and it is growing. There were nearly 900 million 'tourist arrivals' in 2007 (52 million more than in 2006), with tourists spending $733 billion around the world (in 2001 the figure was $463). In the UK alone, nearly 70 million visits abroad were made by UK residents, with Spain the number one holiday destination of choice.

As with all industries, tourism can bring immense economic benefits to the countries involved: an important point when you consider that more than 30% of international tourists visit the developing world. It is the number-one ranked employer in Australia, the Bahamas, Brazil, Canada, France, Germany, Italy, Jamaica and Japan, and the major source of income in Bermuda, Greece, Italy, Spain, Switzerland and most Caribbean countries. Tourism is growing in, or significant to the economy of, eleven of the twelve countries (Brazil, China, Ethiopia, India, Indonesia, Kenya, Mexico, Nepal, Nigeria, Peru, Philippines) that account for 80% of the world's poor.

There are programmes to ensure that tourism benefits the receiving countries, such as the AITO Responsible Tourism Code, the Tour Operators Initiative for Sustainable Tourism Development, and 'Sustainable Tourism – Eliminating Poverty', an initiative owned by the WTO and UNCTAD. In the UK, ABTA is increasingly recognizing the importance of 'responsible tourism' and has been liaising with its membership, pressure groups and the UK Government over how to develop tourism sustainably.

These initiatives demonstrate the presence of ethically responsible tour operators. So, for example, responsibletravel.com enables travellers to find a diversity of pre-screened holidays that will benefit the hosts and their environment as well as the traveller. These holidays are provided by many of the world's leading tour operators, accommodation-owners and grassroots community projects (see www.responsibletravel.com). A Rocha's work in Kenya is a great example of how ethical tourism can help communities (see www.assets-kenya.org).

As positive as these initiatives are, however, they are but a drop in the ocean. The necessity for such special programmes shows that tourism also has negative effects on the receiving countries, particularly in those less economically developed. One of the biggest problems is that often a large proportion of the money generated stays in the tourist-sending countries. By contrast, in some cases as little as 10p of every £1 spent may stay in low-income countries. Tourist demands mean that they may stay in foreign-owned hotels, eating imported food, and visiting attractions with fixed prices arranged by the hotel chain.

Another concern is that of human-rights abuses and the implicit support that a tourist gives a government by travelling to its country. An article in *The Observer* newspaper accused tourists of turning a blind eye to rights abuses and putting bargain holidays before ethical concerns. It cited countries such as Turkey, Indonesia and the Gambia as having poor human-rights records but still attracting tourists in large numbers. In particular, the article accused British travellers of being 'among the most unethical travellers in the world, ignoring global environmental damage and riding roughshod over local populations and their needs'.

Tourism itself can also lead to human-rights abuses. For

example, at the beginning of 1988, pastoralists were evicted from the Mkomazi Game Reserve in Tanzania. Some of their homes were razed to the ground; people received no compensation and were literally left by the roadside with 40,000 cattle. The reason for this was tourism development: to meet the demand for safaris. A recent success story is that of the Nungwi peninsula in Zanzibar, which was under threat of being turned into an international resort, displacing 20,000 people. A campaign headed up by Tourism Concern stopped that happening.

The Beach, a bestseller, was the story of every backpacker's dream to find a place untouched by tourism's destructive hands; the irony being that it was the tourists themselves who brought that destruction. When it comes to environmental issues, tourism has a bad record. A Rocha, was started as a result of the effects of tourism on the Algarve coast, where mass tourism and EC grants led to the destruction of cork-oak plantations, almond and olive orchards and sustainable fishing, replacing them with the rapid (but often unsustainable) profits of hotels, golf courses and marinas.

Environmental problems due to tourism are often most severe in less economically developed countries due to the tourists' demand for a standard of living way above that of the local people and an expectation of luxuries while on holiday. I remember travelling through Rajasthan, when my brother got married in India, and staying in hotels that allowed me to shower every day, while the region was suffering from a drought. Tourism Concern states that a typical tourist uses as much water in one day as a rural villager would use to produce rice for 100 days. Similarly, an eighteen-hole golf course can consume as much water as a town of 10,000 people.

Perhaps the biggest environmental problem facing tourism is how we get there in the first place. Cheaper flights mean that increasing numbers of us are choosing to travel by aeroplane. It is forecast that by 2030 in the UK there will be 500 million plane passengers a year. The problems are immense: climate change from the carbon dioxide emissions (air travel is the fastest-growing source of emissions), health risks from toxic nitrogen oxide emissions, noise pollution, and development pressures with road traffic congestion and greenfield sites tarmacked over for runways and car parks. The harsh reality is that our flying habits need to be severely curtailed, if not stopped altogether.

Throughout this book we are looking at what we can do to see God's justice come in our world. We could be forgiven for thinking that we could take a break from this when it comes to having a holiday! It can be easy to view the money we pay for our holidays as partly paying for insulation from the poverty or environmental damage afflicting the countries we visit, and for the right to ignore the problems of indigenous people: paying for the right to take photos of poverty, but not do anything about it. It is clear that we cannot have that luxury.

There is nothing wrong with holidays. They can be much-needed times of rest and relaxation; times by ourselves or with family and friends; opportunities to see more of our amazing world and the people who live in it. Recent research from ABTA shows that people are becoming more aware of the ethical issues surrounding their holidays and more interested in ensuring that their holidays are responsible. Let's make sure we are among those people.

Action points

- Next time you book a holiday, investigate it fully. For more details on questions to ask your tourist operator, and on campaigning on this issue more generally, contact Tearfund and Tourism Concern.

- Consider your flying habits and, if you fly regularly, look at cutting that down. If your work requires it, try talking to your boss about other modes of transport or methods of communication. Could being 'carbon neutral' become a company policy?
- Does your lifestyle demand regular holidays throughout the year? Think how you might build smaller 'pitstops' into your life to make you less holiday-reliant. Just for once, stay at home instead, giving the money you would have spent to friends who cannot afford to go away so often.
- Take your holiday somewhere that you can get to by boat / train / car. See the journey there as *part of* the holiday, rather than as a way of getting *to* your holiday.
- Holiday with friends you don't see much by visiting them in their homes, whether UK or abroad.

U IS FOR UNWANTED PEOPLES

In this chapter we are going to meet four people. Each one of them illustrates something of the situations faced by the world's most unwanted peoples: refugees.

Kalim came from a country ruled by a dictatorship. Ethnic conflicts and jealousies, provoked by the economic successes of the minority grouping, had led the majority group to use their political strength to gain dominance. Now the minority grouping was facing persecution and oppression. All the men were forced to do hard labour and family members were routinely murdered. One day Kalim saw one of his people being publicly beaten. Enraged by the injustice, he killed the perpetrator. When the dictator learned of this, he tried to kill Kalim. Kalim knew his only option was to flee, and he became a refugee in a nearby country.

Kalim is just one person among many facing similar difficulties. The refugee problem today is vast. Refugees are officially people who are 'outside their country and cannot return owing to a well-founded fear of persecution because of their race, religion, nationality, political opinion or membership of a particular social group'. The latest figures from the Office of the United Nations High Commissioner for Refugees (UNHCR) estimates that there are nearly 10 million refugees. Of these, Afghanistan is the largest country of origin, accounting for some 2.1 million refugees (a fifth of the refugee population). Asia hosts the largest overall population of refugees (48.6%) – with Pakistan hosting 1 million – while Africa hosts 26%. Overall, the developing regions host 7.1 million refugees; 72% of the global refugee population (Europe hosts 16% and America 10%).

War and ethnic conflicts are two of the main factors that cause people to become refugees. The war in Kosovo brought this home forcibly to those of us living in the UK. Suddenly, refugees weren't people on the other side of the world. They looked like us, wore the same clothes as us and needed to be brought into our own country for help. In fact, some friends of ours fostered two 14-year old Kosovan boys who fled the country illegally in the back of a lorry. These boys spoke no English and had witnessed horrors, but they have become a part of our friends' family and have been helped to gain an education and, now, to find employment. The civil war that raged in Burundi, and culminated in the Rwandan genocide in 1994, caused over 500,000 refugees to camp along Tanzania's western border in the most awful conditions, lacking food, water, sanitation and proper shelter, and facing the spread of diseases such as cholera, while the crises in the Darfur region of Sudan and eastern Chad has caused 4.5 million people to be in need of humanitarian aid and led 2.5 million people into refugee camps.

Tamba and his family were facing starvation. Throughout the region, the crops had failed and there was no food. In desperation, Tamba sent his sons to the neighbouring country where there was plenty of food. Through an amazing series of events, his sons met one of the members of the government, who personally gave them permission to bring over the whole family and granted them a special permit to stay until the famine ended.

Families comprise a large proportion of the refugee population. Indeed, around 45% of refugees are under the age of seventeen. Child refugees are extremely vulnerable and the lack of income-earning opportunities forces many children into exploitative livelihoods such as joining fighting forces or prostitution. By contrast, Tamba's sons were exceptionally lucky.

Tamba and his family were forced to seek refuge elsewhere because of wide-scale crop failure. Incredibly, more people become refugees through environmental disasters than for any other reason. It is thought that there may be 25 million environmental refugees today. Most of them are in Sub-Saharan Africa, the Indian subcontinent, China, Mexico and Central America, and it is estimated that by 2050 there could be between 150 – 200 million environmental refugees in the world, due to climate change.

As a high-ranking army officer and best friend of the prince, Amoru was able to enjoy all the luxuries of life. His situation fell apart, however, when his public popularity made him an enemy of the jealous king, who made three attempts at his life. Living in a country that gave him no access to the law, Amoru fled from the capital and became a fugitive in the surrounding hills.

Internally Displaced Persons (IDPs) leave their homes for the same reasons as refugees, but stay within their own country. There are currently nearly 25 million IDPs and they are a subject of huge concern for the international community.

Because they are still under the laws of the state from which they are fleeing they are especially vulnerable, 'falling between the cracks' of current humanitarian law and assistance. In a country in the throes of civil war, much of the basic services may have been destroyed; there may be no well-organized camps to receive IDPs, and fighting may make it difficult for aid organizations to provide relief. Thirteen million IDPs are children who have been forced to leave their homes because of armed conflict or violence. As a Save the Children report stated, 'Once displaced, many children spend at least six years away from their homes. Many live in fear, and are forced to move over and over again.'

Mandelena became a refugee ten years ago with her family. During those ten years she lost both her husband and two sons. Eventually she decided to return to the rural area in her homeland, accompanied only by her daughter-in-law, who insisted on coming with her, although she was from an ethnic grouping different from Mandelena's. On returning home, however, it was clear that the outlook was bleak. Overwhelmed by poverty, Mandelena's daughter-in-law was forced to beg from the men in the fields. Alone, she was vulnerable to sexual abuse.

Voluntarily returning home is generally seen as the best solution for displaced people, and the majority of refugees do prefer to return home if able to do so safely. In 2006, 734,000 refugees went home. Conditions can be very hard, however, if basic infrastructures are still inadequate or ethnic tensions still simmer underneath.

Mandelena's story has a positive ending: she and her mother-in-law were able to return home and a relative still living in the area looked after them. The plight of the majority of women refugees, though, is not so good. Forty-eight per cent of refugees are female and they make up over half of the population in refugee camps (an estimated 13.4 million people are currently in refugee camps). Here they often face worse hardships than the men, rarely having a say in how a camp is run or where services such as water tanks or toilets are sited. While under the care of the UNHCR, three times as many boys as girls receive education.

All the people in our stories were able to find refuge or return home. As travel and communication improve, however, so the number of those seeking remote asylum is increasing. In response, countries are becoming increasingly unwilling to accept refugees. When an emergency situation leads to a massive influx, local communities can find their resources and environment stripped. This happened in the Karagwe district of Tanzania during the Rwandan crisis, when the local people's farms were taken over by huts for the refugees and their trees were destroyed for firewood. It is the poorer countries which bear the brunt of the global refugee problem, and the richer countries should recognize their responsibility to help.

Although the scale of the problem is peculiar to our time, refugees were known in the Bible. In fact, our four stories are all taken from biblical characters: Moses, Jacob and his sons, David, and Naomi and Ruth. In 'A is for Activists' we saw how the laws of the nation of Israel make particular reference to caring for those who are vulnerable, and this includes people from other countries – 'aliens'. Moses' story is especially instructive because it is through the events that he led that the foundation for Israel's laws of compassion was laid. As Deuteronomy 10:18–19 shows, Israel is to love those who are aliens *because* they once were aliens too, in Egypt. Because of God's great compassion for them, so they are to show compassion to others (see also Isaiah 58:7 and Ezekial 22:7).

A wonderful demonstration of this is seen in the early

church. The Christian apologist Aristides gives this description:

They walk in all humility and kindness, and falsehood is not found among them, and they love one another. They don't despise the widow and don't upset the orphan. He who has gives liberally to him who has not. If they see a stranger, they bring him under their roof and rejoice over him, as it were their own brother: for they call themselves brethren, not after the flesh, but after the spirit and in God . . . And if there is among them a person who is poor and needy, and they have not an abundance of necessaries, they fast two or three days that they may supply the needy with their necessary food.

What an encouragement for us to live similarly!

Action point

- Sign up to receive the newsletters of organizations involved in refugee issues: UNHCR or other overseas-development organizations that work with refugee communities abroad (e.g. Oxfam, Christian Aid, CAFOD, Save the Children, Church Mission Society, Médicins Sans Frontières). Allow your increased awareness to lead to other actions such as letter-writing or financial support.

V IS FOR VOLUNTEERS

My next-door neighbour is a vibrant teenage girl who wants to help children with disabilities. While studying childcare at college, she gives one Saturday a month to helping at a playgroup for disabled children and, once a year, takes a week to help with a play-scheme. Lizzie isn't the only person I can think of who gives her time for free. My mum volunteers as a bereavement councillor; one friend does hospital visiting, while another runs a local football team. One neighbour is a Neighbourhood Watch coordinator, and I co-chair our estate's community association. Overall, about 60% of the adult population volunteers, putting in an average of four hours a week, contributing around £40 billion a year to the national economy.

Throughout the course of this book, we have looked at a great many actions that we can take to be reaching for God's justice in our world. Giving our time is a fantastic way of making a difference to the people around us and to the planet on which we live. We could help in a children's club or at a homeless shelter, run a Traidcraft stall at church, work in a charity shop, or help at a lunch club for elderly people. We could use our business skills to help a local charity. We could teach IT, decorate or garden for someone, help run an Alpha group, get involved in local environmental work, help run an arts centre, build, cook, clean . . . The opportunities are endless.

Volunteering is a great way of putting our natural or learnt skills to other uses. It gives us the scope to take the activities that we enjoy and use them for the benefit of others. It is a chance to do something completely different from our paid work.

There are also residential volunteering opportunities. This enables you to try things for a week or two or to dedicate a longer period of time to working with an organization, living away from home. You can spend time with a care organization, an environmental conservation group or a charity dedicated to animal welfare. There are also various Christian opportunities, such as L'Arche homes for people with disabilities, and the Lee Abbey retreat centre.

For something completely different and very rewarding, try volunteering overseas. The traditional time to do this is during a gap year, between school and university, or university and paid work. I went to Malaysia for five months after my A-levels and worked with a Christian care association. The huge range of possibilities, however, means that this needn't be restricted to gap years. Overseas volunteering can be anything from one week to two years, but they will generally involve a cost, and many organizations will expect you to raise your own funds for the trip. Again, there are many Christian opportunities as well as secular ones.

Anybody, anywhere, can be a volunteer. Whether you are young, a student, at home with small kids, disabled, retired or hard at work, there is something for which you can volunteer. Employer-supported volunteering is a good way to help those who are working to find the time to volunteer. The Body Shop, for example, encourages all its staff who work in the head office to take a regular half day to volunteer in the local community. If you're an employer, running a volunteering scheme can be very beneficial. It can lead to improved staff skills and confidence, with higher staff morale; to better team-building and a good public image.

The benefits of volunteering are felt not only by employers who encourage their staff in that direction. Volunteering brings many benefits: the sheer enjoyment of the activity, the satisfaction of seeing results, meeting people, a sense of personal achievement, the chance to learn new skills or gain a qualification, and the opportunity to achieve a position in the community. From a purely selfish motive it also looks great on your CV! Research by Reed Executive found that 70% of top businesses preferred to recruit candidates with volunteering on their CV.

If the statistics are anything to go by, many readers of this book will be volunteers already. If you're not, consider whether you might have some time, however limited, to give. This chapter is perhaps the most practical outworking of all that we have been looking at so far and gives a genuine opportunity to make a real difference to a situation you feel passionate about.

Action points

- Use these questions to help yourself think through what you might like to do:
    1. How much time do you have a week for taking up a new commitment? Is that time in the evenings, at weekends or in the daytime?

2. What do you like doing?
3. What skills do you have?
4. How much responsibility do you want to take on?
5. Are you more focused on local or on national issues?
6. List three local and three national issues that you are interested in. Do you already belong to, or have links with, groups that are taking up these issues?
7. Is there any particular group of people you are interested in?
8. What things do you not like doing?
9. Would you be prepared to put some money aside, either to help a cause or to provide yourself with information? If so, how much?
10. What do other people think about your plans? How will these plans fit in with family life?

- Contact your local volunteer bureau to discuss with them what opportunities there are.
- Get hold of *TimeGuide* from www.timebank.org.uk.

W IS FOR WATER

With UK floods filling our newspapers at one time of the year and hosepipe bans coming into effect at others, we get a small taster of the powerful issue that is water. Yet we think nothing of flushing the toilet, washing our hands, having a shower, filling the kettle . . . Water is, literally, on tap. For those of us living in economically developed countries, it is hard to imagine what it must be like not to have easy access to as much clean water as we like, and almost impossible to grasp that that is the reality for so many people today.

Currently 41% of the world's population (2.3 billion people) live in areas where there is 'water stress'. Out of these 2.3 billion people, 1.7 billion live in high water-stress areas where the consequences of water shortages are more acute, leading to problems with local food production and economic development.

The situation looks set to worsen, and it is thought that by

2025 two out of every three people will live in water-stressed areas. Much of this is due to global demands, which are increasing at more than double the rate of population growth. The biggest share of the world's water goes to agriculture, which consumes 70%, while industry consumes 20%, and the remaining 10% is used for domestic purposes. Unfortunately, agricultural irrigation systems are often inefficient and waste huge amounts of water. Sometimes around 60% of irrigation water is lost to evaporation and runoff, never reaching the crops.

As with so many environmental issues, it is the poor who suffer most but are least responsible for the problems. As competition for water increases, the rich and powerful are the ones who will win. One major cause of water shortages is the migration of people to the cities, leading to a demand that far outstrips supply as people desperately try to survive in slums and shanty towns. As the economic demands placed on poorer countries by the rich nations include the privatization of public amenities, so water prices are hiked up in the cities and the needs of those in urban areas are ignored. Water problems are becoming more severe, too, because of the increasing consumption of water due to economic development and growing standards of living. As we have seen already, the tourism industry can make shortages worse as hotels and golf-courses take most of the water away from the local community. (see 'T is for Tourism'). The health implications are catastrophic, while armed conflict over dwindling water resources, particularly in the Middle East, will become an increasing threat.

In the UK we are fortunate not to suffer extreme water shortages to the extent that other countries do. Water is not, however, the limitless resource that we often think it is. The average person in the UK uses 1,050 litres of water a week and the result is that the natural water-tables are lowering. Not taking into consideration the potential problems that climate change will cause, the National Rivers Authority predicts that by 2021 there will be a deficit in water supply in the Severn Trent, Thames and Anglian regions and, should water demand increase more severely, the Wessex region will also be in deficit.

As well as having a devastating impact on the lives of people around the world, the shortage of freshwater is also severely affecting the ecosystems that rely on it. In the UK, for example, over-extraction is threatening rivers in many regions, leaving water levels too low to sustain their wildlife populations. An English Nature survey found one in ten freshwater wetland Sites of Special Scientific Interest (SSSIs) in England to be threatened by water extraction, and Friends of the Earth have identified over 250 SSSIs in England and Wales that are being similarly affected. Repeated the world over, this is leading to a very worrying decline in the wildlife that these places support. The Freshwater Species Population Index, which measures the average change over time in the populations of 194 species of freshwater birds, mammals, reptiles, amphibians and fish, fell by nearly 50% between 1970 and 1999.

Around the world, it is the building of dams to provide water that is causing the most damage. There are currently 45,000 large dams on the world's rivers. A dam causes huge problems to the hydrological cycle of a river and hence to its ecosystem. The World Commission on Dams found that over 60% of the large dams it surveyed had significant problems with disrupted fish migrations. Alongside dams are the problems associated with providing water for irrigation. Perhaps the best-known example is the Aral Sea in the former Soviet Union, which has shrunk to less than half its original size due to the diversion of two inflowing rivers in order to provide irrigation water for local croplands.

Alongside the issue of water shortage is the extremely pressing problem of pollution and water sanitation. Twenty per cent of the world's population doesn't have access to safe drinking water. The result is that water-borne diseases from faecal pollution is a major cause of illness in developing countries. Polluted water is thought to affect the health of 1.2 billion people, and contributes to the death of 15 million children annually.

In more industrialized countries, a new range of pollutants keeps rivers and underground water supplies contaminated. One of the biggest causes of pollution is intensive agriculture. The large amount of chemicals used means that some of it leaks into groundwater and rivers. Poisonous to wildlife, these chemicals can build up in plants and animals, with the result that those animals at the top of their food chains, such as herons and otters, accumulate high levels of pesticides in their bodies. An increasing problem in industrialised nations is the paving over of natural areas to make paths, driveways and roads. When it rains, the water is not slowly soaked into the ground, but channelled into gutters and storm drains, which contain pollutants from dumped waste. The US Environmental Protection Agency says that this now causes more water pollution than factories and sewage treatment plants.

As with so many of the issues we have looked at in this book, the problems here are huge and often beyond our control. Yet there are always things we can do to ensure that we are playing our part positively.

On a global level, we come back to 'L is for Letters' and our role in supporting the work of organizations by campaigning. This may mean writing to the big water companies, asking them to act responsibly when water is privatized in poorer nations. It might mean writing to our own government, urging them to meet the targets on sanitation agreed at the Johannesburg Summit on Sustainable Development.

At a local level there are steps we can all take to reduce the amount of water we use. We use the most water in flushing our toilets (31%), so finding ways to reduce our usage here will have a major effect. When I was in America recently, staying in an area where water was precious, the toilets had a sign over them that read, 'If it's yellow let it mellow, if it's brown flush it down.' Putting a brick or a 'Hippo bag' in your cistern and buying a dual-flush toilet when replacing an old one will also be effective.

After toilets, the greatest amount of water is used in personal washing (26%), then by washing machines (12%) and then in washing up (10%). With this in mind, we should make sure we shower instead of bath, turn the tap off while brushing our teeth and use our washing machines or dishwashers only when full (or wash up by hand). Water butts, of course, are a great way of saving rainwater for use on the garden; we can also use 'grey' water, in which we've washed ourselves, our dishes or our vegetables.

Access to clean water is the most basic need we have. No wonder the final picture in Revelation is of 'the river of the water of life, as clear as crystal, flowing from the throne of God and of the Lamb' (Revelation 22:1)! All of us need to do what we can to ensure that every person in our world has access, not only to the heavenly water, but also to the earthly 'water of life'.

Action points

- Write one letter that will support the work of one of the organizations on the website regarding water.

- Make a note every time you use water today. Think through what you could do to use less.
- Become aware of your 'virtual water' usage. See www.waterfootprint.org

X IS FOR XENOPHOBIA

The convenience store on my estate used to be run by an Iranian man. After years of harassment he has eventually managed to sell the shop and move on. It was all small-scale stuff: graffiti on the walls, damage done to signs, verbal abuse. The worst thing was an envelope of cockroaches put through the letterbox. Over years, though, it all adds up. Now the shop is run by a Nigerian couple, who are beginning to experience the same things. It can be no coincidence that, of the four shops on the estate, the two run by white people have no problems, whereas Moses' shop and the Indian takeaway suffer constantly.

Xenophobia – or racism – happens all around the globe and is the cause of most of the terrible atrocities that we witnessed last century and this. While in the UK racism is not primarily a 'black versus white' issue, on a global level we have the situation where, as David Haslam says, with its colonial roots 'the poverty line is the colour line, everywhere. Black [or brown, or yellow] almost always means poor . . . white means wealthy.' This fact has been evident throughout the book; so many of the issues that we have been considering, such as HIV or water, predominantly affect people who are not white. Many of us reading this who are white may feel pretty confident that we aren't racist. But one of the challenges of this book is to consider where we may yet be contributing to global racism and how we can begin to change that.

The main focus of this chapter, though, is on racism in the UK. However much the situation may have improved, life on my estate shows me that racism is still alive and well. The UK is becoming increasingly multi-ethnic, with 7.9% of the population coming from ethnic minorities. In England, people from minority ethnic groups make up 9% of the population (compared with only 2% in Scotland and Wales). Nearly half (48%) live in London, where they comprise 29% of residents. In Haringey, the most culturally diverse borough, the council reckons that over 190 languages are spoken. One recent phenomenon is the influx of workers from Eastern European countries. Between 2004 and 2006, nearly 600,000 people came to work in the UK from the eight nations that joined the EU in 2004. 62% of those were Polish. The result of this influx was that Christmas Day 2007 saw more Catholics in church than Protestants for the first time in four centuries!

One important issue for minority ethnic groups in Britain is employment and income. People in minority ethnic groups have higher unemployment rates than people of British descent, and Bangladeshi people have the highest (20% and 24% for men and women respectively). Just over 40% of Bangladeshi men aged under 25 are unemployed, compared with 12% of young men of British descent. Not surprisingly, therefore, Pakistani and Bangladeshi households are more reliant on social security benefits, which make up 19% of their gross income. Overall, people from minority ethnic groups are more likely than people of British descent to live in low-income households. Indeed, almost 60% of Pakistani and Bangladeshi people live in low-income households.

We have a Chinese student from Hong Kong living with us. Last year, as he was walking along the road, he was attacked by a group of white teenagers, for no other reason than for being a 'Chinky'. His injuries put him in hospital. While only 0.3% of white people risk being the victims of a racially motivated incident, 4.2% of Pakistani and Bangladeshi people, 3.6% of Indian people and 2.2% of black people find themselves at risk.

My experiences have all been positive. Alan, our Chinese friend, recently testified in court against his attackers and saw them prosecuted. The family at the centre of the racism directed against the Iranian shop-owner were evicted by the housing association and the main protagonist was sent to prison. Similarly, two men on the estate who were violent towards workers at the Indian takeaway have also ended up in prison as a result.

For many, however, the experience is not so positive. Mal and Linda Hussain, who run a small business on an estate in Lancaster, have faced graffiti, bricks through the windows, fire-bombings, death threats, violent assaults and constant verbal abuse. The authorities have been very slow to react. Mal and Linda began to keep a detailed record of the harassment, recording each incident and logging their calls to the police. Eventually some of the perpetrators began to be successfully prosecuted, although mainly for relatively minor offences. There have now been nearly forty successful prosecutions, but the abuse still continues and none of the perpetrators has yet been evicted from their council home on the estate.[1]

While many problems still persist, overall the situation seems to be improving. A key to this is the media. In February 2002, an encouraging report was published that found that attitudes towards, and the presentation and inclusion of, people from minority ethnic groups have considerably bettered over recent years. The report found, however, that negative attitudes have now shifted on to asylum-seekers. The British media now exhibit some of the most hostile attitudes compared to our European counterparts, and the report criticized the British media for their xenophobic and intolerant coverage of asylum issues.

Those of us reading this will represent many different views regarding Britain's asylum policies. Countries and nationalities are important in giving people a sense of security and identity. If immigration controls are too open and the labour market becomes flooded, the finite resources of the welfare and education system will break down, unable to cope with the numbers. Nevertheless, the fact is that the UK does not receive as many asylum-seekers as some parts of the media claim. Out of fifteen EU countries, Britain ranks eighth in terms of asylum applicants per 1,000 inhabitants. The UK asylum system is far from being a 'soft touch' and has inherent problems, leading to many asylum-seekers' being refused application with no enquiry into whether they might be facing persecution or death when returned home. More positively, refugees and asylum-seekers have much to contribute to the UK, both financially and culturally. A Home Office report estimated that, in 1999/2000, migrants in the UK contributed £2.5 billion, equivalent to saving 1p on the basic rate of income tax.

Despite this, racism demonstrated towards asylum-seekers and refugees can make their lives a misery. Many asylum-seekers arrive in a state of shock or trauma from horrific experiences, yet do not find support on entering the UK. A report by Refugee Action on women's experiences of asylum showed that newly arrived refugee women feel so unsafe in the UK that 83% live under self-imposed curfew, locking themselves indoors by 7pm. Eighty-four per cent live in accommodation with no telephone and 30% have been verbally or physically abused, including being spat on or shouted at. Seventy per cent of refugee women are without a husband, having been separated or widowed by conflict, and 37% of those who are mothers are separated from their children.

In 'A is for Activists' and elsewhere, we have noted the foundational principle that all people have been made in the image of God. One nation, Israel, was explicitly chosen to be 'his people' in order that all nations might be redeemed (Isaiah 49:6). God is manifestly the God and creator of all people, and the Old Testament is not frightened to show God moving beyond the boundaries of his chosen people (for example, in the stories of Ruth and Jonah and in the description of Cyrus, king of Persia, as his 'anointed' [Isaiah 45:1]).

Our supreme model is Jesus, who refused to let racial boundaries stand in the way of God's love (e.g. Matthew 8:5–13; Matthew 15:21–28; Luke 9:51–55 and the parable of the good Samaritan in Luke 10). Writing on 'loving the stranger', the Revd Dr Inderjit Bhogal says, 'Jesus has left an example for his community. Practise hospitality. Eat with each other. Eat with the most vulnerable ones. Eat with "the stranger". Our lifestyle should be one of hospitality and solidarity, not hostility and segregation.' As Abraham showed hospitality to the three strangers in Genesis 18, so we too should be ready to open our doors to those who are not like ourselves. The Chief Rabbi, Dr Jonathan Sacks, quotes the Jewish sages who said, 'On only one occasion does the Hebrew Bible command us to love our neighbour, but in 37 places commands us to love the stranger', and, he adds, 'The stranger is one we are taught to love precisely because he is not like ourselves.' This is hard, and often we fear getting to know people who are different. Yet we need to be willing to try and, regarding asylum-seekers, we must be open-minded as to who is genuine and who is not.

As people following Jesus, racism cannot be something we tolerate. We must all take steps to see it eradicated.

Action points

- Increase your awareness of ethnic minority issues. Keep a lookout for relevant television and radio programmes and sign up to receive a regular paper such as *The Voice, Caribbean Times* or *Asian Times*.
- If 'V is for Volunteering' whetted your appetite, you could consider volunteering for a local asylum-seekers' project or visiting an immigration detainee (see AVID's details below).
- Encourage your church to hold a Racial Justice Sunday each year (usually around September) and, from that, to get more involved in racism issues. For more details contact CCRJ (see www.lisforlifestyle.com).

Endnote

1 A campaign for justice for Mal and Linda is being run by local anti-racists, the Churches' Commission for Racial Justice and the Friends of Mal Hussain (established by the National Assembly Against Racism). For more details, contact Friends of Mal Hussain, c/o NAAR, 28 Commercial St, London E1 6LS.

Y IS FOR YOUNG PEOPLE

One of the primary reasons for setting up the Community Association that I co-chair was to help the young people on our estate. Over a number of years, residents had noticed growing problems from a specific group of young people: drug and alcohol abuse, physical and verbal violence against residents, petty crime and general antisocial behaviour. The problems on the estate are nothing new and have all the classic symptoms, with a high rate of teenage pregnancy, broken families, low education and few prospects, and just plain boredom.

Since writing the first edition of this book, the Community Association has been working hard to see things change. I now chair a Community Action Partnership with the police, local council, youth service and housing association, which ensures that these agencies see the estate as a priority and coordinate their efforts to combat antisocial behaviour. We have had a five-a-side and basketball area built on the green in the middle of the estate and a youth shelter built next to it to provide a place where they can hang out, away from the 'hot spots'. We now have two Community Wardens who work on the estate listening, amongst other things, to what the young people say are their needs. They've set up a Junior Community Warden scheme that works with particular youngsters, encouraging them to participate in estate life and take some responsibility for their area, and two volunteers from the Community Estate run a gardening project that takes young people out onto the green, planting and making the place look nicer. We have a 'Football in the Community' scheme each summer, run by players from Brighton and Hove Albion, which not only teaches football but also focuses on other lifestyle issues, such as health, discipline and respect for others. As I write this, we have just finished a week of open workshops to create a community mosaic that will be laid on the green and it has been wonderful to see lots of young people coming along and joining in.

We haven't expected to work miracles overnight, but at least we have shown the young people that they are worth spending time and money on. In fact it was been real privilege to see the estate changing over the six years that the Community Association has been in existence. The Community wardens have commented on how they now come onto the estate to have a rest, and the social landlord has said he wants to cut his estate walk-rounds from monthly to every-other-month because we 'have turned from being a bad estate into a good estate'.

Of course, the issues on my estate are nothing new and are mirrored around the country. In fact, the problems on my estate are nothing compared with those faced by many others elsewhere. A Department of Health survey of 10,000 5-to-15-year-olds revealed that 10% had a mental health problem.

Three in every 5 children in every classroom have witnessed domestic violence, and 12% of 11-to-15-year-olds report using drugs in the previous year. In an NSPCC survey of 3,000 18-to-24-year-olds, 7% reported abuse and 43% reported bullying.

Perhaps the biggest issue facing our young people is the consumerism that we looked at in 'G is for Globalization' and 'N is for Needs'. Commercialization is getting hold of children from a very young age, leading to the pressures of branding and needing to be part of the MTV generation. Through the marketing of brands comes its sexualization, and there is a constant battle to maintain the innocence and purity of youth.

Whatever the problems, however, there are actions that all of us can take, and none of us lives in an area that is entirely isolated from these issues. Most simply, we can be friendly. How many of us reading this book would cite a youth worker, church leader, neighbour or teacher as having played a large part in our development as children and teenagers, both positively and negatively? One of the most striking aspects of juvenile crime figures is the small percentage of young people who commit the highest number of crimes. What a difference could be made if these young people were able to form relationships with people who would help them through life![(1)]

When I was little, my mum looked out of her front window one winter's day to see two young girls standing out in the snow. When they were still there some time later, Mum went out and talked to them, and discovered that their mum had shoved them outside first thing in the morning and told them not to come back till evening. Mum invited them inside, and that was the start of a friendship with them that lasted all the way through their teens. They still pop in from time to time to say hello. They have had a rough life, but I wonder what else might have happened to them had they not had my mum to be a steady influence as they grew up.

It is also good for adults to remember that young people are more than capable of being a positive force for good themselves and are very good at making a difference. Cred, for example, ran a conference on human rights in Westminster for schools in London. Two sixth-form students, in particular, found the topics interesting and decided to volunteer to help at future events. This led to their chairing a conference – attended by Gordon Brown, Hilary Benn (Minister for International Development) and Jan Vandemoortele (of the UN Development Programme) – which looked at how to reach the UN's Millennium Goals of halving child poverty by 2015.

In the UK we are facing the problems of a population consisting of too few young people and too many old people. In many places around the world, however, the reverse is the case. In fact, the current generation of people under eighteen is the largest in the history of the world; more than a fifth of the world's population is aged between ten and nineteen. When one considers that about 85% of adolescents live in developing countries, and that 600 million children and adolescents grow up in families surviving on incomes of less than 70p ($1) a day, it becomes clear that the problems faced by young people are immense.

In 'H is for HIV', we saw the shocking statistic that AIDS will eventually kill half of all fifteen-year-old Ethiopian, South African and Zimbabwean boys. Indeed, every fifty seconds a child dies of an AIDS-related illness, and another becomes infected.

AIDS is not the only health issue facing young people across the world. Every day, on average, more than 26 000 children under the age of 5 die, most of them from preventable causes. Water sanitation issues, which we looked at in 'W is for Water', and malnutrition, caused by poverty, are majority factors in these deaths. Measures that we take for granted – such as immunization, an emphasis on breastfeeding and the consumption of iodized salt (to combat iodine deficiency disorders that leads to mental impairment) – are crucial in seeing the health of our world's young people improve (and encouragingly are improving).

Running parallel to issues of health is the issue of education. Although primary-school enrolment is increasing, still 115 million primary-school-aged children are out of school (60% of them girls). In Somalia, only 12% of children attend primary school. It hardly needs to be said how important good education is, both to the well-being of the individual – developing qualities and giving them skills that can help them avoid dangers such as bonded labour or armed recruitment – and to the development of a country, which can be transformed in a single generation when education is improved.

Crucial to both the health and education of young people is the status of women in a society. It is no coincidence that, looking at a map showing women's literacy rates, nearly all the countries with under 30% are in Africa (In Burkino Faso and the Niger a shocking 90% of women are illiterate). Where women are valued, girls are valued, and where girls are valued, the education and health of all young people are improved.

Young people face many hazards today. Armed conflict places young people in extremely vulnerable positions.(2) Issues around young people working – whether in sweatshops, bonded labour or in the sex industry – continue to cause untold damage to millions of lives.(3)

Whether it is these issues or others, such as street children, the underlying problem is the same: poverty. It is a sad fact that a young person's prospects for survival and development depend on where he or she was born. In particular, external debts have a direct impact as money is taken away from health and education and from fighting the other problems young people face. To see the lives of young people around the world set free from the tyranny of fear and deprivation, we must push for the cancellation of unsustainable debt (with strings attached to ensure the money reaches those most in need). We must press for developed countries to increase their aid budget to countries locked in poverty, and for macro-economic and fiscal policies to make young people a key focus.

The good news is that, wherever there are young people in trouble, there are people working to see matters change. One woman I know has moved out to South Africa to work with babies abandoned on the streets of Johannesburg. Cred supports a primary school in the slums of Addis Ababa, Ethiopia, that has been specifically set up for street children. Between 1998 and 2003, money from our supporters has enabled 600 children to attend that school. Another of our partners, Women at Risk, also in Addis Ababa, works with young prostitutes, giving them vocational and life-skills training and helping them to move out of the sex trade. There is so much that needs to be done, but also so much that is being done to see situations change. We can all be a part of it.

Action points

- Think about the young people in your neighbourhood or church. Are their needs and potential being met? Is there anything you can do, even if it's just being a friendly face? Perhaps 'V is for Volunteering' has already inspired you to do something!

- If you do not already do so, consider supporting an organization that works with young people, whether at home or abroad. The list is endless, but we've met some organizations already in other chapters: e.g. Cred ('A is for Activists'), Phoenix Community Care ('X is for Xenophobia') and HopeHIV ('H is for HIV'). See also the Viva Network (details on website).

Endnotes

1 This is happening, for example, with regards to school exclusion. Cornerstone Church in Swansea runs a highly effective programme working with young people identified as most likely to be excluded.

2 More than 2 million children died, and over 1 million children were orphaned or separated from their familes, in the last ten years as a direct result of armed conflict; and an estimated 300,000 children are serving in armed forces, as soldiers and servants, many being forced into sexual slavery. Each year about 6,000 children are killed or injured by landmines.

3 About a million children (mostly girls) are caught up in the commercial sex trade, while 250 million children in developing countries work, many in hazardous and exploitative labour. Basic rights are often overlooked. Ninety per cent of domestic workers (the largest group of child workers in the world) are girls between 12 and 17 years old.

Z IS FOR ZEITGEIST

On a CD cover recently I read this:

'What is 'Zeitgeist?' *we are continually quizzed.* 'Spirit of the time', *we nod, trying to look the part.* 'Era defining', *we occasionally add as a bit of a try on. We'll tell you what it is . . . It's trying to make some sense of this glorious mess'.*

Throughout this book we have been 'trying to make some sense' of 'this glorious mess' that is our world. 'Glorious mess' wonderfully encapsulates what we see as we consider the many different topics that make up this book.

There is no doubt that we live in a beautiful world. Just consider the amazing beauty of the rainforests or the coral reefs; the skylark spiralling above the fields, the prairie dog scurrying along the ground or the water vole swimming through the rivers. As humans, too, we have been richly blessed with the ability to form friendships and nurture our families; with the means to travel and trade throughout the world, creating wealth and prosperity; with opportunities to develop our talents and potential, enhancing our sense of well-being.

This most certainly is glorious. As we see continually, these blessings come from God who loves giving us good things. As we use them well, so the glory goes back to him.

But we also live in a mess. The spirit of the age blinds us to the origin of these good things, turns us away from our relationships and into ourselves, and causes us to see these gifts as being our own, to be used for our own ends. As with the good, so with the evil. It runs through every chapter of this book: greed and exploitation, selfishness and idolatry.

As people who don't want to conform to the spirit of the age, but want to be transformed by the renewing of our minds (Romans 12:2), we must look critically at the blessings we have received and ensure that we are using them to bless others. The danger is that we can become hypnotized by our cultural norms and blinded to the possibilities we have to see change.

The good news is that there *is* an alternative. The gospel has the power to break that hypnotism and enables us to change our lives so that they may reflect the goodness of God and his blessing for his creation. In essence, what we are talking about here is moving from the spirit of the age to the kingdom of God, pictures of which we have looked at a number of times. As we do this we move from the values of this age and towards the values of the kingdom: values of selflessness and peace, of inclusivity and love.

The kingdom of God is made visible through our prayers; through the concentrations of our worship; through our practice of the disciplines and the cultivation of the Christian virtues. The kingdom is also made visible on this earth through our actions. Each time we can be bothered to send off a campaign postcard, each time we look up and smile at a neighbour, each time we buy a fair-trade product or take the trouble to leave the car at home, we are playing our part in seeing God's kingdom come, now and into the future.

This book has been a call to change our lives in order to respond to the many challenges facing our world. The changes facing us are many and varied: for some they are easily implemented while for others they demand wholesale adjustments. Whether we decide to write a campaigning letter every month, move our investments, sell our car, give more of our money away, change our eating/shopping habits or revolutionize our working situation – whether these decisions we make take us a month to carry out or the rest of our lives – the gospel of Jesus fills us with hope and with the confidence that these changes are worth making. By making them we are building into God's promised future, when there will be no more sickness or suffering, tears or death, and when all of God's creation will freely worship him.

NOTES

Full details of works cited are provided in the Bibliography at www.lisforlifestyle.com.

Introduction

Financing Energy Efficiency: Lessons from Brazil, China, and Beyond, pp. 25–26.

M. Northcott, *A Moral Climate: the ethics of global warming*, p. 50.

A is for Activists

J. A. Motyer, *The Prophecy of Isaiah*, pp. 461, 478–482.

R. Valerio, *The Inspirational Jesus: Jesus, the Kingdom and Social Justice*.

C. J. H. Wright, *Living as the People of God*, pp. 82–83.

The New Internationalist (November 2001), p. 19.

2002 Report from the New Policy Institute (with support from the Joseph Rowntree Foundation).

J. Moltmann, *Theology of Hope*, p. 2.

P. Kuzmic, 'Eschatology and Ethics: Evangelical Views and Attitudes', in V. Samuel and C. Sugden (eds.), *Mission as Transformation*, p. 151.

www.poverty.org.uk, www.npi.org.uk (accessed 1.02.08).

US Census statistics 2007 (www.census.gov).

B is for Bananas

Fairtrade information in this chapter comes from the Fairtrade Foundation

The New Internationalist (October 1999).

Ethical Trading Initiative, *Annual Report* (2001/2002).

Ethical trading standards taken from the Base Code of Labour of the Ethical Trading Initiative.

Christian Aid's 'Trade for life' material.

C is for Creation

C. J. H. Wright, *Living as the People of God*, pp. 68–69.

L. Osborn, *Guardians of Creation*, p. 29.

C. J. H. Wright, *Old Testament Ethics for the People of God*, pp. 117, 119

W. J. Dumbrell, *Covenant and Creation*, p. 34.

C. Gunton, *Christ and Creation*, p. 64.

R. Valerio, 'Chainsaws, Planes and Komodo Dragons: Globalization and the Environment', in R. Tiplady (ed.), *One World or Many?*.

D. Wilkinson, *The Message of Creation*, p. 261.

R. Bauckham and T. Hart, *Hope Against Hope*, p. 137.

D is for Driving

Much of the information for this chapter comes from Friends of the Earth's paper, *Road Transport and Air Pollution*, and from *The Ecologist*, *Go M.A.D!*

The Ethical Consumer (December 2000/January 2001), p. 10.

West Sussex County Council, *Connections* magazine (summer 2001).

D. McClaren, S. Bullock and N. Yousuf, *Tomorrow's World*, pp. 117–118.

Statistic on average car costs comes from the RAC.

McClaren et al., *Tomorrow's World*, p. 113.

US Department of Transportation, Research and Innovative Technology Administration.

US car figures taken from the Union of Concerned Scientists (www.ucsusa.org).

A Rocha supporters' magazine (July 2005).

Cycling figures from the Office for National Statistics.

E is for Energy

D. McClaren, S. Bullock and N. Yousuf, *Tomorrow's World*, p. 85.

The New Internationalist (June 2001), p. 12.

US statistics for 2006 from the Energy Information Administration website (www.eia.doe.gov).

McClaren et al., *Tomorrow's World*, p. 86.

Sobrino quote from M. Northcott, *Life After Debt*, p. 66.

M. Northcott, *A Moral Climate*, pp. 49, 96.

N. Spencer and R. White, *Christianity, Climate Change and Sustainable Living*, p. 51.

The Ecologist, *Go M.A.D!*, p. 57.

F is for Food

Soil Association Briefing Paper, *Pesticides Allowed Under SA and UKROFS Organic Standards*.

For more information on Lindane see the Soil Association's policy paper, *Lindane and Breast Cancer: Why Take Risks?*

Soil Association, *The Truth About Food*.

J. Humphrys, *The Great Food Gamble*, ch. 1.

Soil Association, *The Truth About Food*.

For the details on the positive health benefits of organic food see the Soil Association's report, 'Organic Farming, Food Quality and Human Health' (can be found on their website).

M. Van Straten, *Organic Living*, p. 31.

H. Fearnley-Whittingstall, *The River Cottage Cookbook*, p. 209: a fantastically inspiring book.

For more on salmon, see 'K is for Kippers'.

The National Farmers' Union.

Friends of the Earth, *Real Food: Time to Choose'*, pp. 6–7.

W. Berry, 'The Pleasures of Eating', in M. Schut (ed.), *Simpler Living, Compassionate Life*, p. 106.

For one attempt to enhance the relationship between food and time, see www.slowfood.com.

M. Schut, 'Food as Sacrament', in *Earth Letter* (November 2001), p. 11.

Organic sales figures from the Soil Association's 2007 Market Report and the US Organic Trade Association's 2007 Manufacture Survey (www.ota.com).

Food and Agricultural Association of the United Nations, *livestock's long shadow: enviromental issues and options*, pp. 22, 290.

G is for Globalization

My writing on globalization started in the form of three Tearfund Policy Papers: *Globalization and the Poor*; *Globalization, the Church and Mission* and *A Biblical Perspective on Globalization*. The material in this chapter draws on those papers and on other writing and speaking that I have done on this subject, including two chapters in Tiplady, *One World or Many?*. My fullest writing on globalization is now in the form of a Cred Paper entitled

Globalization and Poverty. To obtain a copy contact Cred (see 'A is for Activists' for details).

I. Linden, in C. Reed (ed.), *Development Matters*, p. 3.

Department for International Development report on globalization, *Eliminating Poverty: Making Globalization Work for the Poor.*

LEB, p. 81.

M. Moore, 'Trade Rules for Global Commerce', *Global Future* (First Quarter, 2001), p. 2.

'Of Celebrities, Charities and Trade', *The Economist* (1 June 2002).

For two excellent defences of globalization see J. Micklethwaite and A. Wooldridge, *A Future Perfect*, and P. Legrain, *Open World*.

N. Klein (2000), *No Logo*, London: Flamingo.

P. Legrain, *Open World*.

P. Heslam, *Globalization*, p. 25.

S. Escobar, 'The Global Scenario at the Turn of the Century', in W. Taylor (ed.), *Global Missiology for the Twenty-first Century*.

A. Araujo, 'Globalization and World Evangelism', in Taylor (ed.), *Global Missiology*, p. 60.

H is for HIV

Unless otherwise stated all statistics are taken from the '2007 AIDS Epidemic Update', jointly produced by UNAIDS and WHO. I think it is good to note that in 2001 there were 40 million people with HIV so we can see that global efforts to combat this virus is having some impact, although the problems are, of course, still immense.

The New Internationalist (December 1993), p. 18.

G. Paterson, 'HIV/AIDS: A Window on Development', in C. Reed (ed.), *Development Matters*, pp. 45–46.

The New Internationalist (December 1993), p. 13.
Acet UK, 'HIV / Aids Update' (July 2000).
My thanks to Adrian Gosling, trustee and former Director of HopeHIV, for the action points.

I is for Investments

Triodosnews (editions 8 and 9).
P. Mills, 'Faith *versus* Prudence?', 'Investing as a Christian' and 'Interest in Interest' have all provided invaluable biblical material for this chapter.
EIRIS can provide a full list of financial products.

J is for Jobs

J. Dominguez and V. Robin (*Your Money or Your Life*, pp. 229–230) would go further. They state that the only purpose served by paid employment is getting paid, and stress that the other personal aspects are all equally available in unpaid activities.
Ellen Goodman quote cited in J. Luhrs, *The Simple Living Guide*.
M. Greene, 'Supporting Christians at Work (without going insane)', p. 13, citing the '1999 Survey of Managers' Changing Experiences' from the Institute of Management.
P. A. Marshall, 'Work', in D. J. Atkinson et al. (eds.), *New Dictionary of Christian Ethics and Pastoral Theology*, p. 899,900.
J. Stott, *Issues Facing Christians Today*, p. 166.

K is for Kippers

Y. Kura, L. Burke, D. McAllister and K. Kassem, 'The Impact of Global Trawling'.
Environmental Justice Foundation, *Squandering the Seas*.
The Marine Conservation Society factsheets.

Food and Agricultural Association, *The State of World Fisheries and Aquaculture 2006*.

For a good account of the effects of salmon farming, see the chapter on 'Fear of Fish: Fish Farming', in J. Humphrys, *The Great Food Gamble*.

Soil Association press release, 'No such thing as a free lunch in salmon farming'.

The paragraph on prawn farming comes from G. Mock, R. White and A. Wagener, 'Farming Fish: The Aquaculture Boom', p. 3.

Salmon industry figure taken from the Scottish Salmon Producers' Organisation website (www.scottishsalmon.co.uk) accessed 7.2.08.

For more on the the situation in the North Atlantic see the websites of the International Atlantic Salmon Research Board (www.nasco.int) and the International Council for the Exploration of the Sea (www.ices.dk)

MSC Annual Report 2006/7.

The Cooperative Bank's *Ethical Consumerism Report 2007*.

L is for Letters

Printed letter is from a union leader in the Dominican Republic, campaigned for by Amnesty International.

M is for Money

Some of this chapter's material also appears in J. Odgers and R. Valerio, *Simplicity, Love and Justice*.

C. Blomberg, *Neither Poverty Nor Riches*, p. 83.

D. Kraybill, *The Upside-down Kingdom*, pp. 114–129.

Thanks to Phil Wall for the 'luxury tax' idea.

N is for Needs

James Jones, *Jesus and the Earth*, p. 25.

T. Sine and C. Sine, *Living on Purpose*, pp. 138–139 and 40.

N. T. Wright, *For All God's Worth* (page number unknown).

The action points have been taken from J. Odgers and R. Valerio, *Simplicity, Love and Justice*.

O is for Organic

Living Earth, the magazine of the Soil Association (April/June 2002).

Office of National Statistics, 'Average Weekly Expenditure by UK Households, 2006'.

Earth Matters, the magazine of Friends of the Earth (autumn 2000), p. 13.

For recipes for both cleaning products and beauty products (and a whole host of other organic things), check out www.care2.com, a great website.

The Ethical Consumer (April/May 2002), p. 16.

Culpeper (www.culpeper.co.uk), Green People (www.greenpeople.co.uk), Logona (logona.co.uk), Neal's Yard (nealsyardremedies.com) and Weleda (www.weleda.co.uk) are all good companies to look at for organic beauty products.

M. Van Straten, *Organic Living*, p. 15.

P is for Paper

Unless otherwise indicated, all the information in this chapter comes from Rainforest Action Network fact-sheets.

Paper usage statistics come from *The Ecologist*, *Go M.A.D!*, p. 110. US statistics from the Paper Industry Statistics webpage of TAPPI (the Technological Association for the Worldwide Pulp, Paper and Converting Industry): www.tappi.org.

Friends of the Earth, *Disappearing Forests*.

For more information on how to buy 'good wood', see the *Good Wood Guide* from Friends of the Earth.

Economic Research Service of the US Department of Agriculture (www.fas.usda.gov).

Rainforest Action Network, 'Call for an Immediate Moratorium on U.S. incentives for agrofuels, U.S. agroenergy monocultures and global trade in agrofuels'.

See Friends of the Earth UK for indepth reports on the issue of palm oil plantations.

Q is for Questions

D. Clark, *The Rough Guide to Ethical Living*, p. 46. He is not arguing for localisation himself, merely making the point.

Oxfam press release, 27.2.08.

A. Leopold, *Sand County Almanac*, p. 197, cited in, S. Bouma-Prediger, *for the beauty of the earth*, p. 16. The full quote is, 'one of the penalties of an ecological education is that one lives alone in a world of wounds'.

R is for Recycling

Unless otherwise stated, the material for this chapter all comes from Friends of the Earth literature.

UK rubbish statistics are from 2004 and are taken from the DEFRA (Department for Environment, Farming and Rural Affairs) website. They were the most recent stats available in 2008.

2007 statistics from DEFRA (www.defra.gov.uk) and Friends of the Earth.

2006 statistics from the Environmental Protection Agency (www.epa.gov).

The Ecologist, Go M.A.D!, p. 155.

The research on toxic landfill sites was published in the medical journal the *Lancet* (8 August 1998), pp. 423–427. For more information, see www.foe.co.uk/pubsinfo/infoteam/pressrel/1998/19980807122119.html.

EF Schumacher quote cited in J. Odgers and R. Valerio, *Simplicity, Love and Justice*, p. 52.

The Ecologist, *Go M.A.D!*, pp. 101, 155, 157.

2007 statistics from DEFRA (www.defra.gov.uk) and Friends of the Earth.

S is for Simplicity

The bulk of this chapter is based on material in J. Odgers and R. Valerio, *Simplicity, Love and Justice*.

T. Sine, *Mustard Seed versus McWorld*, p. 128.

R. McCloughry, 'Community Ethics', in D. J. Atkinson et al. (eds.), *New Dictionary of Christian Ethics and Pastoral Theology*, p. 110.

M. Schut (ed.), *Simpler Living, Compassionate Life*, pp. 50–51, 253.

It has been pointed out to me that alongside silence, solitude and contemplation stand the complementary triad of intercession, community and the Word of God. I find this helpful and hope that these are reflected elsewhere in the book.

Henri Nouwen, 'Contemplation and Ministry', in Schut (ed.), *Simpler Living, Compassionate Life*, p. 54.

R. Foster, *Freedom of Simplicity*, pp. 8–9, 14.

T is for Tourism

The size of the tourism industry depends on the world situation. In times of war, or increased instability, the arms trade is the biggest industry.

Tourism statistics come from the World Tourism Organization (WTO) and the Association of British Travel Agents. 'Tourist arrivals' is the term used to measure tourism

Tearfund, *Worlds Apart*.

C. Ashley, *Pro-Poor Tourism Strategies: Making Tourism Work for the Poor* (Overseas Development Institute, 2001).

For more details on ABTA and responsible tourism see the 'responsible tourism' page on their website, www.abta.com, and read their paper: ABTA and Tearfund, 'Improving Tour Operator Performance: The Role of Corporate Social Responsibility and Reporting'.

The Observer (27 October 2001).

Tourism Concern website. TC has been at the front of raising awareness of tourism issues.

For more details on A Rocha's work, see their contact details in 'C is for Creation' at www.lisforlifestyle.com.

Research from Brunel University, cited in Tourism Concern, *In Focus* (winter 1996).

John Spellar MP, Transport Minister (9 April 2002).

ABTA Package Holidays Survey (2002).

U is for Unwanted Peoples

The 1951 Geneva Refugee Convention.

UNHCR, *Statistical Yearbook 2006*, pp. 7–11.

UNHCR, *Statistical Yearbook 2001*, p. 13.

Sudan/Chad statistics from Oxfam's website (www.oxfam.org.uk).

Save the Children, Liberia Emergency Update (September 2002).

UNHCR 2007, from website: www.unhcr.ch.

UNHCR, 'World Refugee Overview' (from website).

Oxfam, 'Asylum Facts', from website: www.oxfam.org.uk.

Save the Children, 'War brought us here: protecting children displaced within their own countries by conflict' (2000).

V is for Volunteers

Institute for Volunteering Research (www.volunteering.org.uk), 'Helping Out: a national survey of charitable giving and volunteering' (2007).

TimeGuide, published by TimeBank in association with the National Centre for Volunteering, p. 13.

1997 National Survey of Volunteering.

The Ecologist, *Go M.A.D!*, p. 152.

The questions in the *Action Points* are taken from R. McCloughry, *Taking Action*, p. 23, and from *TimeGuide*, p. 6.

W is for Water

C. Revenga, 'Will There be Enough Water?', taken from the EarthTrends website, earthtrends.wri.org, using figures from the World Resources Institute in collaboration with the University of New Hampshire.

UNEP, 'Vital Water Graphics: Executive Summary', taken from the UNEP website, www.unep.org.

Earthtrends website of the World Resources Institute (www.earthtrends.wri.org), accessed 20.02.08.

Tearfund, 'Water Matters' campaign material.

The Ecologist, *Go M.A.D!*, p. 158.

D. McLaren, S. Bullock and N. Yousuf, *Tomorrow's World*, pp. 185–186, 188–189.

C. Revenga and G. Mock, 'Freshwater Biodiversity in Crisis', taken from the EarthTrends website.

UNEP, 'Vital Water Graphics', nos. 24, 25, 26, 27.

C. Revenga and G. Mock, 'Dirty Water'. www.epa.org.

X is for Xenophobia

D. Haslam, *Race for the Millennium*, p. 210.

National Statistics, 'Minority Ethnic Groups in the UK' (2002), p. 1–3.

BBC News, 22.8.06 (news.bbc.co.uk)

The European Monitoring Centre on Racism and Xenophobia's report on Racism and Cultural Diversity in the Mass Media. See www.eucm.at/publications. The EUMC became the EU Agency for Fundamental Rights in 2007.

Refugee Council, 'Nailing press myths about refugees, introduction' (2002), taken from website, www.refugee council.org.uk/news/myths/myth001.htm. This article by the Refugee Council is a helpful challenge to some of the most common negative assumptions made by the media.

'Frequently Asked Questions' on the Refugee Council's website.

C. Gott and K. Johnston, *The Migrant Population in the UK: Fiscal Effects*'.

Refugee Action, *Is It Safe Here?*, p. 1.

Racial Justice Sunday pack, 2002.

J. Sacks, *Faith in the Future*, p. 78.

Y is for Young people

From a presentation given by S. Gallimore, then Head of Child Protection for East Sussex.

Barnardo's literature (2001).

UNICEF, *The State of the World's Children 2000*, pp. 68, 72, 74.

UNICEF, *Annual Report 2000*, pp. 4, 14.

International Action Against Child Poverty (IAACP), *Grow Up Free from Poverty*, p. 31 (using UNAIDS' figures from 2001).

UNICEF, *Annual Report 2008*, p.6.

UNICEF, *State of the World's Children 2001*, pp. 68–69, 70–71

UNICEF, *State of the World's Children 2002*, pp. 78, 42, 52.

UNICEF, *State of the World's Children 2007*, p. 6.

UNICEF 2005 statistics for Somalia (www.unicef.org/infobycountry/somalia/html).

Z is for Zeitgeist

'Zeitgeist: New wave club culture' (Stress Recordings), 1997.
B. Goudzwaard, *Globalization and the Kingdom of God*, p. 68.
N. T. Wright, *New Heavens, New Earth*, p. 22.